"Folk Dancing"

[by]
Mary Bee Jensen
[and] **Clayne R. Jensen**

**Brigham Young
University Press**
[C 1973]

Library of Congress Cataloging in Publication Data

Jensen, Mary Bee.
    Folk dancing.

    Published in 1966 under title: Beginning folk
dancing.
    Bibliography: p. 143
    1. Folk dancing. I. Jensen, Clayne R., joint
author. II. Title.
GV1743.J4 1973   793.3'1   73-4771
ISBN 0-8425-0458-3

Library of Congress Catalog Card Number: 73-4771
International Standard Book Number: 0-8425-0458-3
© 1973 Brigham Young University Press. All rights reserved
Brigham Young University Press, Provo, Utah 84602
New, enlarged edition. Fourth printing 1978
First edition © by Wadsworth Publishing Company, Inc.
Printed in the United States of America

1980 1Mp 48801

Contents

1.
Discover
Values

Folk dancing is an invitation and an opportunity for you to learn more about your foreign neighbors: to help you understand their customs and beliefs; to teach you about their history and geography; to give you insight into the joys of their daily living—joys that have been handed down through the years; to help you discover the backgrounds of the countries and the people; and to help you appreciate the cultural heritage your ancestors have passed on to you.

The language of the folk dance is common throughout the world; communication is established through the rhythms of the dance. People of different countries find it easy to forget their differences when they dance together during such events as the international folk-dancing festivals of Europe. Folk dancing helps to scale the barriers of international problems and unite members of the group.

Watching the dancers—the English with their typical country dances, the Hungarians with their fiery rhythms, and the Yugoslavs with their precise and delicate footwork—arouses in you a curiosity about these people, their history, and their civilization as a whole.

Folk dancing, therefore, opens up many avenues for learning. As an activity, too, it is immediately satisfying. Its values, carried over into your life, can provide many enjoyable hours—challenging you, the individual dancer, as well as the dance group. Participation in this activity may well provide you with an absorbing interest that will remain with you for a lifetime.

Why is folk dancing so popular with individuals and groups throughout the world? Why is it included in educational programs at many levels? Specific answers to these questions are given in the lists of values that follow.

SOCIAL VALUES

1. Folk dancing is highly social in nature because you, the dancer, change partners often during many of the dances;

even when two of you perform as a couple, each of you is also a member of the dance group.

2. Because of its social nature, folk dancing helps to break down shyness, making it easy for you to develop new friends with mutual interests.

3. Folk dancing gives you a chance to mingle with the opposite sex in a wholesome recreational activity that fosters a desirable pattern of conduct.

4. As do other forms of dance, the folk dance encourages you to develop courtesy, etiquette, and other social attributes that contribute to your ability to meet and talk with others.

5. Because folk dances represent the cultures of many different countries, the dance sessions take on a cosmopolitan atmosphere that lends personality to the occasions.

6. As a wholesome leisure-time activity, folk dancing is especially important now because leisure time is more abundant than ever before in the United States.

7. The cosmopolitan heritage of the folk dance encourages you to learn about people of other countries.

PHYSICAL VALUES

1. Folk dancing helps you develop rhythm, neuromuscular coordination, balance, grace, and poise.

2. Its social nature encourages you to groom yourself well, dress appropriately, and make yourself as attractive as possible.

3. Folk dancing is strenuous enough that, if you do it regularly, it will contribute to your physical fitness. Many experts agree that such exercise is essential to good health. Folk dancing has an advantage over many activities in that you can enjoy it for most of your life.

PSYCHOLOGICAL VALUES

1. Folk dancing affords you, as well as the other participants, the satisfaction of achieving. You enjoy learning new skills and developing new techniques. Achievement in enjoy-

able activities contributes to your permanent satisfaction and well-being.

2. The satisfaction of being accepted into social groups of your choice, which folk dancing offers, contributes to your psychological stability and adjustment.

3. The importance of wholesome and interesting hobbies to your mental health and social adjustment has been pointed out by several leaders in the field of psychology, among them the eminent J. B. Nash. Folk dancing is the primary hobby of many people.

4. Folk dancing is an activity through which you may become truly recreated—refreshed emotionally, physically, and mentally. It can help bring your life into balance, adding adventure and joy to an otherwise routine day.

These values that folk dancing offers will come in greater measure to you as you dance skillfully and develop a deep appreciation for the dance. People tend to select activities which they enjoy and perform well, and to avoid those that they perform poorly. Therefore, as the development of skill adds to your enthusiasm for folk dancing, the activity serves you better.

This book is designed to help you develop skill rapidly so that folk dancing may quickly become meaningful and enjoyable to you.

The dances chosen from twenty-three countries to be included in this text represent a unique cross section of styles and techniques to give you a broader understanding and appreciation of the folk cultures of your neighboring countries.

2.
Know Folk-Dancing History

Dancing has always been a part of man's life. Historians tell us that many drawings left by cavemen on the walls of their caves depict leaping actions characteristic of dance movements. Vases recovered from ancient Egyptian tombs show dancers in flowing dance movements. In these same tombs, Egyptian carvings on wood show men dancing to depict happiness.

When primitive man danced, he was performing rituals that he considered necessary to fulfill his basic needs. Pantomime played an important part in his dance rituals, for he would act out through movement what he wanted to happen. If the village people needed rain for their crops, they would use hand movements to mimic the falling of the rain. Their basic needs were for food, health, strength, and victory in war. Their pleas for all of these were integrated into their dances.

Later, more civilized men gathered together in rural villages that were highly protected and somewhat isolated. Their primary source of recreation was dancing. People danced for many reasons and on many occasions. Almost any time that people gathered together—whether for planting or harvesting, or for housewarmings or weddings—dancing became a part of the occasion. Village dances were performed over and over, with the older generation teaching native dances to the younger people. Gradually, within each country, a symbolic dance became associated with the culture of the people.

To the alert folk dancer, the characteristics of a dance portray the personality of the culture in which the dance developed. For example, the Cossack dances of Russia, which are fast and strenuous, indicate a vigorous people. The beautiful ballroom dances from Poland reveal a proud and exacting personality. The tarantellas from Italy, which are fast and exciting, show the changing temperaments of the Italian dancers. The Swiss couple dances tell the story of young couples entering into courtship, while the Lithuanian dances illustrate the agricultural activities of their people. Greek chain dances honor the people's religion; and the kolo dance displays characteristics of the Yugoslavians, particularly the

Serbians. The exciting czardas demonstrates the flavor of the Hungarian national dance form. The Alpine people of Bavaria and the Tyrol perform their Schuhplattlers with clapping, stomping, and kicking. In North German dances, the dance formations are the typical characteristic. Couple dances play the most significant role. England is known for her country dances with their intricate pattern work, as well as for her famous war dances, of which the sword dances are the best known. Finally, our own American folk dances have found their place in the folk dance world, country square dances the most prominent of our contributions.

The oldest forms of folk dancing come from areas of the world where civilization was first developed; the growth of civilization has brought an accompanying growth of the folk dance movement. America is one of the latest additions to the folk dance world, and Israel, since becoming an independent country in 1948, has contributed significantly to the large collections of folk dances.

As your experience increases in the field of the folk dance, you will develop a greater appreciation for all types of dancing. As a beginning dancer, you will find the fast rhythms of the Ukrainian dances particularly appealing. As you gain experience and confidence, you will find the complex rhythms of the Balkan dances to your liking. Remember that folk dances have been passed down through the generations for a particular kind of enjoyment and are not to be changed as other dance forms are. As you learn a Russian dance, you should also learn the proud carriage of the body and the exactness of the steps. And when you perform the Philippine Tinikling, be light-footed and at ease with the steps as are the island dancers. From the history of each dance, attempt to interpret its meaning and significance in the culture where it was developed.

3.
Improve Dancing Techniques

Learning the correct steps is an important part of folk dancing. But to further improve your dancing, you must become aware of other basic fundamentals associated with the dance. Practicing rhythm, styling, etiquette, body carriage, and posture and systematically memorizing patterns are all part of learning to dance well. Good costuming can also add much to the spirit and atmosphere of an evening of dancing.

RHYTHM

How do you become conscious of rhythm? First you must feel the beat of the music. Most music has a common basic meter of either 2/4, 4/4, 3/4, or 6/8. As you listen to the music, clap your hands or tap your foot in time with the beat. Listen and hear how the beats of the music are grouped into rhythmic patterns, usually moving from four measures to eight measures, then to 16, 32, etc. This grouping of measures of music forms a pattern that will lead you through a dance sequence. Folk dancing differs from social and square dancing in that the sequence of dance steps is fixed, and the rhythm of the music provides the cues.

If you try to memorize dance patterns by counting the steps in them, you will be dancing to arithmetic rather than music—and making hard work of an easy task. It is better to listen to the music and let its rhythm do the counting while you learn the dance steps.

STYLING

The style of a dancer has a dual meaning in the folk dance field. Basically, it refers to the appearance an individual makes while dancing. It includes posture, carriage, ease with which you perform the step patterns, rhythm, and general appearance. To make a good appearance on the floor, you must always apply one rule—stand tall. Reflect your enjoyment of the dance by displaying a proud carriage of the body and a pleasant smile.

A second meaning of styling applies specifically in the field of folk dancing. As you master the dances from the different countries, you become more aware of the nationality of a specific dance. Mastering the different types of national styling should be a goal of all folk dancers. Movies, study of ethnic groups, and good instruction on styling all help you achieve this goal.

ETIQUETTE

Consideration for others at all times is prime in folk dance etiquette. Many people learn more slowly than others and feel self-conscious about their dancing. Since self-confidence is important to good dancing, a considerate person will help others gain confidence.

When a dance calls for close cooperation between you and your partner, you must try to perform your steps in a way that makes it easier for your partner to dance with you. Avoid roughness. In many of the couple dances, each individual is a soloist for part of the dance, and he is dependent upon his partner for the other parts. Each of you should perfect your own technique so that your partner will have confidence in you. Then both of you can relax and enjoy the routines.

Since folk dancing is a strenuous form of dancing, you should give special attention to personal cleanliness. A good deodorant is a must, and washable shirts or blouses are better attire than woolen sweaters.

BODY CONTROL

Folk dancing is excellent training for good body control, poise, and balance. As the dances progressively become more difficult, your need for control and balance increases. Adequate strength is fundamental to good body control and, therefore, is also fundamental to many of the vigorous dances. Walking is good conditioning for these dances. Also, lead-up dances or exercises are important before you move into some of the more strenuous dances.

MEMORIZING PATTERNS

Folk dancing is more fun if you can see rhyme or reason to a dance sequence. Since every dance follows a specific pattern, it is important that you approach the learning of patterns systematically. You need to evaluate the dance and to develop a system for remembering it—one such as that given for "Sweets of May" (p. 95) for instance. At the first look, "Tinikling" may seem like a prohibitive dance to learn. But when you observe that steps 1, 2, 3 are followed by two steps that are different, then by steps 3, 2, 1, you have a mental picture to guide you through the sequence. Even the most difficult and challenging dances can be simplified by such a memorization pattern.

Dancers who come into a group with the idea they can't dance are their own worst enemies. Therefore, take a positive attitude, enjoy yourself, get acquainted with your fellow dancers, and learn to find the pleasures in folk dancing.

4.
Learn
Basic
Skills

To fully enjoy folk dancing, you must become acquainted with its basic skills. This chapter contains information to help you learn the dances readily and to appreciate the meaning of each one.

BASIC TERMINOLOGY

First, you must learn the terminology of the folk dance. Terms that are used over and over to describe dance movements are abbreviated, thus:

W	woman	bwd	backward
M	man	ct	count
R	right	LOD	line of direction
L	left	RLOD	reverse line of direction
ft	foot	meas	measure
cw	clockwise	#	number
ccw	counterclockwise	pt	point
fwd	forward	&	and

BASIC DANCE POSITIONS

Second, learn basic dance positions. The correct position for a dance is often clarified by a demonstration given by the instructor. However, you should know the names of the dance positions so that you can better understand the teacher's explanations and demonstrations. Eight of the more common positions used in folk dancing are illustrated here.

Upper left:
Closed Ballroom Position
Partners face each other; M places R hand at small of W's back and extends L hand to side, shoulder height. W places L hand on M's R shoulder, puts R hand in M's L hand.

Upper right:
Semi-Open Position
Partners face LOD with M's R and W's L sides together. Hold hands as shown in closed position.

Left:
Open Position
Partners face LOD, with inside hands joined. Outside hands may be at waist or, for W, holding skirt.

15

Upper right:
Shoulder-Waist Position
A very typical folk
dance position. Partners
face each other, and W
places her hands on M's
shoulders, keeping arms
almost straight. M
places his hands on W's
waist. Partners lean
slightly away from each
other.

Right:
*Variation of the Shoul-
der-Waist Position*
Partners take shoul-
der-waist position, and
each moves to L until R
hips are adjacent. In
many dances, M then
places his R hand on
W's waist and L hand
on her R arm just above
the elbow.

Upper right:
Square Dance Swing Position
Partners stand with R hips close together, facing opposite directions. The man places his R arm around W's waist and holds her R hand in his L hand. W places her L hand on M's L shoulder.

Upper left:
Promenade Position
Both dancers face LOD with W on R of M. They join R hands and L hands. R hands are above L hands.

Left:
Varsouvienne Position
Partners face LOD with W on R of her partner and slightly forward. W raises her hands to shoulder height, and M holds her R hand with his R and her L hand with his L.

17

BASIC DANCE FORMATIONS

Third, learn basic dance formations. You must know the terminology of basic dance positions, formations, and step patterns if the group practice sessions are to be efficient. It takes only a few seconds for the group to assume the correct formation if each dancer has a clear mental picture of that formation. The following illustrations show the basic formations for the dances included in this book.*

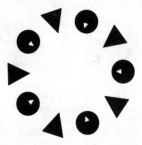

Single circle facing the center.

Single circle facing forward, ccw.

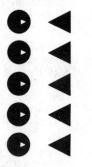
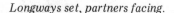

Longways set, partners facing.

Single circle with partners facing.

*Circle=W; triangle=M; point=facing forward.

18

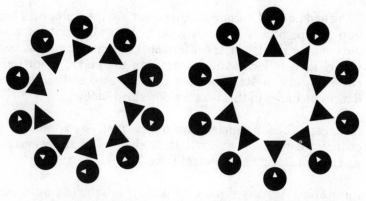

*Double circle facing cw,
W on the outside.*

*Double circle with partners facing,
M on the inside.*

*Double circle with M facing cw,
W facing ccw.*

*Square dance position, No. 1,
couple with back to music.*

*Sets of three facing three,
M between two W.*

19

The fundamental forms of movement are the walk, run, leap, hop, jump, skip, slide, and gallop. A combination of these movements results in specific step patterns. The most commonly used folk-dancing patterns are the polka, schottische, two-step, and waltz. The step patterns used in the different dances included in this text are described below.

Balance: When balancing toward partner, step fwd on R, change weight from L to R (ball change). Step away from partner on L, changing weight from R to L.

Buzz Step: Usually done with partner in shoulder-waist position. Step R (ct 1), push with L toe (ct &).

Cut Step: Displacement of one ft with other. Standing on L ft, swing R ft fwd. Then swing R ft back and step exactly where L ft was, as L ft swings back. Repeat, swinging L ft fwd and displacing R ft.

Grapevine: This may be started by stepping to R with R ft, or moving to R by crossing L over R. Step R to R, step L in front of R, step R to R, bring L ft behind R. Repeat sequence.

Pas de Basque: With R ft, leap diagonally R (ct 1). Step on ball of L ft in front of R toe (ct &). Step in place with R ft (ct 2, &). Repeat, starting with L ft.

Polka: Hop L (ct &), step R (ct 1), step L ft beside R ft (ct &), then step R (ct 2). Repeat, starting with R ft. Basic count: Hop, step, close, step.

Russian Polka: No hop in the Russian polka. It is more like a fast two-step. Leap R (ct 1), close L to R (ct &), then step R (ct 2, &). Repeat, starting with L ft. Count: leap, run, run.

Heel-Toe Polka: Hop on R ft, extend L heel to L side; hop on R ft and place L toe by R heel, then polka to L. Repeat, extending R heel to side. Count: Heel, toe, hop, step, close, step.

Promenade: Partners, R hand in R hand over L in L, facing ccw, walk around the circle.

Push Step: Move to R. Place weight on L toe, step sidewards to R with R ft (bend R knee slightly as though falling onto R ft). Bring L toe to side of R ft and repeat.

Schottische: Step R fwd; bring L to R; step R fwd, hop R; swing L ft slightly fwd. Repeat, starting with L ft. Count: Fwd, 2, 3, hop (three steps and hop).

Step-Hop: Step L, then hop on L. Step R, then hop on R.

Toe-Heel-Touch-Kick: Rhythm is 1-2-3-4. Hopping on L ft 4 times, place R toe to R side (ct 1), place R heel in same spot (ct 2), point R toe in front of L toe (ct 3), kick R ft diagonally R, knee high (ct 4). Repeat sequence, hopping on R ft and touching L toe. This step is common in Russian dances.

Two-Step: Rhythm is 1 & 2 &. Step R ft fwd, bring L ft to R, step R ft fwd and hold (pause). Repeat, starting with L ft. Count: Step, close, step (pause).

Waltz: Step fwd L, sideward R, close L to R (taking weight on L). Step bwd R, sideward L, close R to L (taking weight on R). Repeat. (Box waltz.)

Dances Using Basic Steps and Patterns

When looking for a dance with a specific step pattern that you wish to learn, use the following list as a guide. If one dance step forms the major part of a particular dance pattern, the dance is listed under that step.

Walk: Galopede, Hier Ek Weer, Tant' Hessie.

Two-Step: Misirlou, To Tur, Ziogelis.

Polka: Cotton-eyed Joe, Doudlebska Polka, Kalvelis, Raksi Jaak.

21

Schottische: Korobushka, Lowland Schottische, Salty Dog Rag.

Dances consisting of other step patterns: The predominant steps used in these dances are listed in parentheses. Alunelul (side, behind, side, stomp); Corrido (grapevine, step-draw, soldado); D'Hammerschmiedsg'selln (step-hop); Hopak (pas de basque, Russian polka, push step, prysiadkas, buzz step); Kreuz Koenig (mazurka, landler run); Maori Stick Game (hand and eye coordination skills); Mayim, Mayim (grapevine); Sauerlander Quadrille (Neheimer step); Tinikling (waltz, tinikling step); Vayiven Uziyahu (run, bounce, leap); Sweets of May (7's and 3's, skip change of step). Ersko (side-behind, schottische); Jessie Polka (toe-touch, polka); Uzicka Carlama (fwd & back, side-together, clicks); Pod Borem (pas de basque, clicks); Czardas Vengerka (side-together, Bokazo, skip-behind); Hambo (waltz, hambo turn); Shepherd's Crook (strathspey, highland fling).

5.
Choose from Folk-Dancing Categories

FROM SIMPLE TO DIFFICULT

This section includes thirty-five different dances arranged progressively from simple to more difficult. The dances are classified into three general categories: beginning, intermediate, and more advanced. They were especially selected for your enjoyment. They have proven popular among folk dancers all over the world.

Following is the list of dances, the country in which each dance originated, the dance formation, and the page on which the dance description is given.

Full descriptions of each dance are provided for initial learning. These descriptions contain explanations of the steps and the step patterns. Briefs are provided for use after the dance has been taught. They help the dancer to recall quickly the content and pattern of each dance. The teaching hints are provided to assist the dancer along the path of faster and easier learning and to give future aid to the prospective teacher.

Beginning

Intermediate

Misirlou	Greece	Line	54
Lech Lamidbar	Israel	Single circle	55
Vayiven Uziyahu	Israel	Line	57
Mayim, Mayim	Israel	Single circle	59
Korobushka	Russia	Double circle	61
Lowland Schottische	Scandinavia	Double circle	63
Ziogelis	Lithuania	Two threesomes facing	66
Raksi Jaak	Estonia	Threesome	69
Oslo Waltz	England	Single circle	71
Pod Borem	Poland	Double circle	73
Sauerlander Quadrille	Germany	Square	75
Czardas Vengerka	Hungary	Double circle	78
Salty Dog Rag	America	Double circle	80

More Advanced

Hambo	Sweden	Couples anywhere	82
Kreuz Koenig	Germany	Two-couple circle	85
Hopak	Russia	Double circle	88
Corrido	Mexico	Double circle	92
Sweets of May	Ireland	Square	95
Shepherd's Crook	Scotland	Threesome	98
Tinikling	Philippines	Couple facing	102
Maori Stick Game	New Zealand	Couple facing (seated)	106

BY NATIONALITY

The following list has been arranged according to nationality in order that a student may conveniently find dances from a particular country. The abbreviations B, I, and A indicate beginning, intermediate, and more advanced levels.

AFRICAN
    Hier Ek Weer (B)
    Tant' Hessie (B)

AMERICAN
    Cotton-eyed Joe (B)
    Jessie Polka (B)
    Salty Dog Rag (I)

Choose from Folk-Dancing Categories

CZECHOSLOVAKIAN
    Doudlebska Polka (B)

DANISH
    To Tur (B)

ENGLISH
    Galopede (B)

ESTONIAN
    Raksi Jaak (I)

GERMAN
    D'Hammer-
      schmiedsg'selln (B)
    Kreuz Koenig (A)
    Sauerlander Quadrille (I)

GREEK
    Misirlou (I)

HUNGARIAN
    Czardas Vengerka (I)

IRISH
    Sweets of May (A)

ISRAELI
    Lech Lamidbar (I)
    Mayim, Mayim (I)
    Vayiven Uziyahu (I)
    Ve' David (B)

LITHUANIAN
    Kalvelis (B)
    Ziogelis (I)

MEXICAN
    Corrido (A)

NEW ZEALAND (Maori)
    Maori Stick Game (A)

PHILIPPINE
    Tinikling (A)

POLISH
    Pod Borem (I)

ROMANIAN
    Alunelul (B)

RUSSIAN
    Hopak (A)
    Korobushka (I)

SCANDINAVIAN
    Lowland Schottische (I)

SCOTTISH
    Road to the Isles (B)
    Shepherd's Crook (A)

SCOTCH-ENGLISH
    Oslo Waltz (I)

SWEDISH
    Hambo (A)

YUGOSLAVIAN (Serbian)
    Ersko Kolo (B)
    Uzicka Carlama (B)

6.
Perform
Selected
Folk
Dances

The thirty-five dances described in this chapter are arranged progressively from easy to more difficult.

The learning hints at the end of each dance will promote faster and easier learning now and will give future aid if you are a prospective teacher.

ALUNELUL

This dance, meaning "little hazelnut," was introduced by Dick Crum at the Folk Dance Camp in Stockton, California.

Pronunciation: Ah-loo-*neh*-loo.

Nationality: Romanian.

Record: Folk Dancer MH 1120.

Meter: 2/4.

Steps: Sideward step, stamp.

Formation: Single circle, facing center, with hands on shoulders of the person next to you. Keep facing center throughout dance.

Pattern in Brief
1. Five steps and two stamps.
2. Three steps and one stamp.
3. Step, stamp; step, stamp; step, stamp, stamp.

Repeat entire dance.

Pattern

Meas
1–2	Introduction, no movement.

I

1–2	Step R to side, cross L behind R, step R to side, cross L behind R. Step R and stamp L heel beside R twice (no weight).
3–4	Repeat, starting with L ft and moving to L (opposite footwork).
5–8	Repeat from beginning.

II

1	Move R by stepping R, crossing L behind, and stepping R. Stamp L heel.
2	Move L by stepping L, crossing R behind, and stepping L. Stamp R heel.
3—4	Repeat meas 1—2.

III

5—8	In place, step R, stamp L; step L, stamp R; step R, stamp L twice. Repeat action with L: step L, stamp R; step R, stamp L; step L, stamp R twice.

Repeat entire dance.

Hints for Learning

This is a good dance for learning to move lightly on your feet as you progress sideward. The stamps are light, and the entire dance should look effortless as you perform it. Remember to listen carefully to the music.

VE' DAVID

Ve' David is a simple dance that has the quality of movement and music so typical of the people of Israel. A translation of the title means: "David of the beautiful eyes." It was composed by M. Shelom. Rivka Sturman, a top choreographer of the Israeli dance, taught the dance to Miriam Lidster of Stanford University.

Pronunciation: Vee-Dah-vee.
Nationality: Israeli.
Record: Festival-Symphony FS 201 LP.
Meter: 4/4.
Step: Walk.
Formation: Couples in double circle, open position and facing ccw. Inside hands joined and held low.

Pattern in Brief
1. Walk fwd 4, back out into single circle 4.
2. All into center of circle 4 and back out 4 (raise arms up and lower them).
3. Girls into center of circle 4 and back out 4 (men clap 8 times).
4. Men into center 4 (clap 4), turn to face girl on R of partner, walk fwd 4 and swing 8 (buzz step).

Repeat entire dance.

Pattern

Meas
1—4	Introduction, no movement.
1	Beginning R, walk fwd 4 steps moving ccw around circle.
2	With 4 steps M back out to L side of W to form single circle. W take 4 steps in place, turning to face center of circle.
3—4	Walk to center of circle in 4 steps, raising joined hands slowly to shoulder height. Back out 4 steps as arms are lowered.
5—6	W walk 4 steps to center raising arms to shoulder height and return with 4 steps. M stand in place and clap rhythm.

7   M walk toward center of circle 4 steps, clapping 4 times. W stand in place. On ct 4 M makes R turn and looks at W on R of original partner.

8   M walks to this W with 4 steps and takes her for his new partner.

9—10   Take shoulder-waist position: R hips adjacent; W places R hand on M's R shoulder, L hand on M's L shoulder; M places R hand on W's waist and L hand on her R arm. Buzz-step turn for 8 counts (2 meas). Repeat dance with new partner.

Hints for Learning

Buzz Step: The group forms a single circle, facing ccw. Imagine you have your right foot on a scooter. As you move around the circle you push with the L foot. The teacher should clap the rhythm and gradually increase the tempo. Try to do the step in place, turning R. Then take your partner in shoulder-waist position (move so that R hips are adjacent). Practice the buzz-step turn.

TANT' HESSIE

Tant' Hessie, a South African dance meaning "Aunt Esther's white horse," was presented at the University of the Pacific Folk Dance Camp in 1962 by Huig Hofman of Antwerp, Belgium.

Pronunciation: Tahnt-Hessy.
Nationality: South African.
Record: Folkraft 337-006B.
Meter: 2/4.
Steps: Walk, buzz-step turn.
Formation: Double circle, partners facing, M on inside.

Pattern in Brief
1. Walk fwd 4 (R shoulders), walk back 4 to place.
2. Walk fwd 4 (L shoulders), walk back 4 to place.
3. Do-sa-do (pass R shoulders) with 8 walking steps.
4. See-saw (pass L shoulders) with 7 walking steps. On 8, step L and call HEY.
5. In shoulder-waist swing position, buzz-step turn for 16 steps, using dip down on R, up on L.

Repeat entire dance, moving L to new partner.

Pattern

Meas

1—4 Introduction, no movement.

I

1—2 Beginning L, walk 4 steps toward partner with R shoulders adjacent (forms single circle).
3—4 Walk 4 steps back to place.
5—8 Repeat action of meas 1—4 with L shoulders adjacent.

II

1—4 Do-sa-do with partner with 8 walking steps, passing R shoulders.
5—7 See-saw with partner with 7 walking steps, passing L shoulders.

8   Step toward partner on L ft, extend arms, and call HEY.

III

1—8   Swing with partner: take shoulder-waist position, and then step so that R sides are adjacent. M moves L hand up to hold W's upper R arm. Starting on R ft, buzz-step turn cw with a slight dip on the R ft (it has the feeling of down-up-down-up). End swing with M's back to center of circle.

Repeat entire dance, with M progressing to W on L.

Hints for Learning

Tant' Hessie offers a chance to experiment with a basic walk. The music invites a slight swagger and a natural swinging motion of the arms. This is also one of the finest dances for getting acquainted with group members.

HIER EK WEER

"Here I am again" is the translation for this happy mixer from South Africa. Shirley Durham learned the dance while teaching in Europe and later brought it back to the United States.

Pronunciation: Heer Eck Veer.
Nationality: South African.
Record: Windsor 7141A.
Meter: 4/4.
Steps: Walk, buzz step, stamp.
Formation: Double circle, M inside facing cw, W facing ccw.

Pattern in Brief
1. 16 walking steps, M cw, W ccw; reverse for 16.
2. Both facing ccw, move fwd and clap own hands, clap partner's hands, clap own hands, clap partner's hands, clap own hands for 5. Buzz-step turn with partner for 8 buzz steps.
3. Repeat second sequence.

Repeat entire dance.

Pattern

Meas

1—2   Introduction, no movement.

I

1—4   M walk 16 steps cw as W walk 16 ccw, M L; W R.
5—8   Reverse line of direction, M walking 16 steps ccw, W walking 16 steps cw. M pass original partner and take next W for new partner. Both face ccw.

II

1—2   Moving fwd ccw, clap own hands, clap partner's hands, clap own hands, clap partner's hands, clap own hands five times. On ct 4 of second measure take shoulder-waist swing position with R hips adjacent.

3—4   Buzz-step turn for 8 steps. M finish with back to center.

5—8   Repeat meas 1—4.

Repeat entire dance, changing partners with each full dance sequence.

Hints for Learning

Hier Ek Weer has an interesting musical arrangement and is a good dance for practicing a basic walk to rhythm. Use this dance as a mixer.

DOUDLEBSKA POLKA

This polka was introduced at Michael Herman's Folk Dance Center in New York and has since become a favorite throughout the folk dance world.

Pronunciation: Dŏod-leb-ska.
Nationality: Czechoslovakian.
Record: Folk Dancer MH3016.
Meter: 2/4.
Steps: Polka, walk.
Formation: Couples in shoulder-waist position anyplace on floor.

Pattern in Brief
1. 16 polkas in LOD.
2. Form stars.
3. M in circle face center and clap while W polka around outside.

Repeat entire dance.

Pattern

Meas

1—4   Introduction, no movement.

I

1—16   Take 16 polkas, LOD, anywhere on floor. M hop R, step L, close R, step L. W start L. Partners turn cw as they move ccw around dance floor.

II

1—16   M make L-hand star, retaining hold of partner with R arm around her waist. W's L hand is on M's R shoulder. (It is preferable to make many small stars rather than one large star. If all M go into one star, put L hands on L shoulders of M in front.) Polka around singing "Tra-la-la-la-la-la-la-la " to rhythm of music.

III

1—16 M face center and clap own hands twice on cts 1, &. On ct 2, extend hands to side and clap hands of M on each side once. W reverse LOD (cw) and take 16 polka steps around circle of M as they clap. When music starts over, M dances with W behind him.

Repeat entire dance with new partner.

Hints for Learning

Polka: An easy way for the group to learn the polka is to form a single circle, facing the center. Then do the following: (1) Slide six times facing center of circle; turn R with a hop and slide six times facing the wall. Turn L to face center and repeat this sequence. Use the same technique, doing only four slides, then do it with only two slides. (2) Perform the two slides progressing ccw around the hall. (3) Repeat the second routine in time with a polka record. While practicing the step, slowly eliminate the definite turn from center to wall.

Right Turn: In order to effectively execute a R turn, the group faces one wall. Each dancer turns his head to look at the wall on his right, then turns and faces that wall. The group repeats this until each dancer has made a complete turn. Now take partners, M facing the original wall. Hold hands and look at your own R wall and turn so that you face it. Repeat until a full circle has been made. Use shoulder-waist position and repeat with sliding steps. Polka turn R.

An additional hint for making right turns is to demonstrate how the M steps in front of the W on the first step of the polka. The M makes a definite half-turn, then the W makes a half turn. The W leans back from the waist and keeps her arms relaxed but straight out from the M's shoulders.

COTTON-EYED JOE

This American folk dance, passed down from our pioneers, fits most polka records and offers a chance to experiment with a polka step.

Nationality: American.
Record: Imperial 1045.
Meter: 2/4.
Steps: Heel-toe polka, turning polka, push step.
Formation: Large double circle of couples in two-hand position (use elongated hold: join hands; extend arms at shoulder height). M back to center.

Pattern in Brief
1. Heel-toe polka.
2. Separate (making individual circles).
3. Push steps.
4. Partners polka.

Repeat entire dance.

Pattern

Meas

1—4   Introduction, no movement.

I

1—2   M hop R, touch L heel to side; hop R, touch L toe
       to R heel; take one polka step to M's L. W use
       opposite ft pattern.
3—4   Repeat, starting with opposite ft.
5—8   Separate from partner; M turn L, W turn R with 3
       polka steps; on meas 8 stamp three times. M places
       thumbs in belt front, W holds skirt out to side.

II

1—2   Take 4 push steps with M and W moving around
       circle ccw. M weight on R toe, W on L toe. M push
       onto L ft, W onto R ft. M places hands, palms out-
       ward, on back hip pockets. W holds skirt out.
3—4   Take 4 push steps in opposite direction (cw).
5—8   In shoulder-waist position, take 4 turning polka
       steps. Make two R turns (cw) as you move ccw
       around the circle.

       Repeat entire dance.

Hints for Learning
Refer to the Doudlebska Polka step (page 37). To practice
the push step, form a single circle, facing center. With weight
on L toe, step onto R with slightly bent R knee. Then bring L
toe to instep of R ft and repeat the push. A two-step can be
used for this dance, but most dancers seem to enjoy it more
with the polka step, which allows them to move more
quickly around the floor.

ROAD TO THE ISLES

The Scottish bagpipes add a delightful touch to this slow and easy schottische. This dance was brought to the United States by Phillip Aldrich.

Nationality: Scottish.
Record: Imperial 1005A, Folk Dancer MH 3003, Folkraft 1095.
Meter: 2/4.
Step: Schottische.
Formation: Couples in double circle, in varsouvienne position, facing ccw.

Pattern in Brief
1. Point L and grapevine R, point R and grapevine L; point L fwd and back.
2. Two schottische steps fwd, turning on second step-hop; one schottische step back, turning on step-hop; stamp three times, R, L, R.

Repeat entire dance.

Pattern

Meas

Introduction, three chords.

I

1	M and W point L toe fwd and hold.
2—3	Grapevine to R starting with L ft back of R, R ft to R, and L ft in front of R.
4	Repeat meas 1, starting with R ft point fwd.
5—6	Grapevine to L starting with R ft back of L, L ft to L, and R ft in front of L.
7	Point L toe fwd and hold.
8	Point L toe back and hold.

II

9-10	Schottische fwd starting with the L ft.
11-12	Schottische fwd starting with the R ft. On the step-hop make a R turn to reverse LOD. W is now on M's L.

13-14   One schottische step, traveling reverse LOD; on hop turn L to face ccw. Retain hand hold on turns.

15-16   Stamp lightly in place R, L, R.

Repeat entire dance.

Hints for Learning

When learning the schottische, some dancers have difficulty with the step-hops. The step-hop resembles a skip and can be practiced as a single teaching unit. After the step-hop is learned, combine the step, step, step, hop. Add the four step-hops to the two schottische steps and your sequence is: Step, step, step, hop—step, step, step, hop—step, hop, step, hop, step, hop, step, hop.

An additional practice is to change the steps into slightly running steps which give a feeling of excitement and fun to many of the schottische dances.

ERSKO KOLO

The translation means "the villager." It was first taught by Rickey Holden.

Pronunciation: *Air*-sko-Kolo.
Nationality: Serbian.
Record: Folkraft F 1498.
Meter: 2/4.
Steps: Side-behind step, schottische step.
Formation: Circle dance, no partners.

Pattern in Brief
1. 14 side-behind and step-stamp to R; repeat to L.
2. Schottische step diagonally fwd and bwd, then fwd and bwd facing center. Repeat.

Repeat entire dance.

Pattern

Meas

1—2   Introduction, no movement.

I

1—7   14 side-behind (start R to side, L behind R).
8   Step R, stamp L (no weight on L ft).
9—16   Repeat pattern 1—8, reversing direction (step L to side, R behind).

II

1—2   One schottische step diagonally R starting with R ft (ccw).
3—4   One schottische step diagonally backward (cw). Reverse original schottische step of meas 1—2.
5—6   Facing center, one schottische step toward center.
7—8   Still facing center, one schottische step backward.
9—16   Repeat pattern 1—8.

Hints for Learning
Steps in the first part move very quickly. Practice using the ball of the ft to support the weight of the body. The schottische steps of the second part are done very slowly in comparison to the side-behind steps.

hands and move one position up the set to repeat dance with new head couple.

Hints for Learning

You may use a skipping step instead of the polka for the two-hand swing and the polka-down-the-center. You can learn this easy dance in a matter of minutes.

UZICKA CARLAMA

This dance comes from the town of Uzice in Yugoslavia.

Pronunciation: Oozh-itch-kah Char-lah-ma.
Nationality: Serbian (Yugoslavian).
Record: Folkraft 1498.
Meter: 2/4.
Steps: Step-close, sideward click, kolo pas de basque.
Formation: Single circle.

Pattern in Brief
1. Forward, back, close.
2. Hop-clicks sideward with kolo pas de basque for direction change.

Pattern

Meas

I

1	Step R ft fwd; step bwd on L ft in place (1 &).
2	Step R ft beside L (2 &).
3—4	Repeat pattern of meas 1—2 starting with the L ft.
5—16	Repeat meas 1—4 three more times (total 4 times).

II

17	Step R, close L.
18	Two hop-clicks. (Hop on L ft and click heels together moving R).
19—22	Repeat 17—18 twice (total 3 times). (Count: side together, click, click, side together, click, click, side together, click, click.)
23	Step R to R side; close L taking weight on L.
24	Three steps in place, R, L, R (kolo pas de basque).
25—32	Repeat 17—24 moving to the L (L, together, click, click, etc.).

Hints for Learning

The "clicks" present a learning problem for some dancers. Raise the R ft about 8 inches to the side and at the same time hop and left L ft up to touch R ft. Practice continuous clicks until the "lift" is mastered. Holding hands in a single circle gives added support.

KALVELIS

Kalvelis, a dance of the middle nineteenth century, originated in Lithuania soon after the polka was introduced there. It represents a transition between the older, slower dances and the new, spirited ones that adopted the polka. Kalvelis means "little smith," and the hand-clapping in the refrain represents the striking of hammer on anvil. This is one of many Lithuanian dances introduced to America by Vyts Beliajus.

Nationality: Lithuanian.
Record: Folkraft 1418.
Meter: 2/4.
Step: Polka.
Formation: Single circle, W on R, hands joined.

Pattern in Brief
1. Polka in circle R, then L. Chorus.
2. W into center and back, M into center and back. Chorus.
3. Grand R and L. Chorus.
4. Polka with partner around circle. Chorus.
5. Polka anywhere, alternating with chorus to end of record.

Pattern

Meas

1—2	Introduction, no movement.

I

1—7	Beginning R ft, polka in circle to the R for 7 polkas.
8	Stamp three times L, R, L.
1—8	Repeat meas 1—8, beginning with L ft and moving to the L.

Chorus:

9—10	Face partner, still in single circle. Clap R hand into own L hand (as though hitting an anvil), clap L hand into own R, clap R hand into own L, clap L hand into own R (clap on each ct).
11—12	Hook R elbows with partner and turn once around with 4 step-hops or 2 polka steps.
13—14	Repeat meas 9—10.
15—16	Hook L elbows with partner and turn once around

with 4 step-hops or 2 polka steps.

17—24   Repeat meas 9—16.

II

1—3   Facing center of circle, W dance 3 polka steps toward center of circle. M clap. (Count: 1 & 2 (pause), 1 & 2 (pause), etc.)

4   Stamp 3 times, turning R to face partner.

5—7   Polka back to place with 3 polka steps.

8   Stamp 3 times, turning R to face center.

1—8   Repeat sequence of 1—8 with M going into center and back and W clapping. Use more vigorous step and heavier stamping.

9—24   Chorus.

III

1—16   Extend R hand to partner in single circle for grand R and L. Pass one person per polka step. Take person for chorus at end of last meas.

9—24   Chorus.

IV

1—8   In shoulder-waist position, 8 polka steps around the circle, turning cw as you progress ccw.
Repeat polkas (meas 1—8).

9—24   Chorus.

Polka anywhere around the room with partner until end of record. (Alternate with chorus.)

Hints for Learning

When learning Kalvelis, first form a mental picture of its sequence of five step patterns. The first, fourth, and fifth step patterns all use polka steps in a circle. In the second pattern, W go to the center and back, then M do the same. The third is a grand R and L.

D'HAMMERSCHMIEDSG'SELLN

This dance, originally for men only, was presented by Vyts Beliajus, and has proved to be a most popular dance. Its name means "the blacksmith's apprentice." Coordinating the arm movements presents a personal challenge to the dancers.

Pronunciation: D'hammer-schmitt Gzelln.
Nationality: German.
Record: Folkraft 1845x45B.
Meter: 3/4.
Steps: Step-hop, waltz.
Formation: Two couples side by side facing own partners.

51

Pattern in Brief
1. Clap pattern with partner.
2. Circle L and R (step-hop).
3. Clap pattern: M1 with W2 and M2 with W1 (diagonally across).
4. R- and L-hand stars (step-hop).
5. Clap pattern, M2 and W1 leading off.
6. Waltz anywhere (Landler waltz).

Pattern

Meas

1—4   Introduction, no movement.

I

1—16   Clap pattern: Clap own thighs with both hands, clap own chest, clap own hands; clap partner's R hand with your R, clap partner's L hand with your L, clap both hands with partner. (Variation on clap pattern: make individual R turn as you clap thighs, chest, and own hands.)

II

1—8   Two couples join hands to make circle. Move cw with 8 step-hops (M L, W L).

9—16   Reverse circle and move ccw with 8 step-hops.

III

1—16   M 1 and W 2 start clap pattern with each other on ct 1 of meas 1. M 2 and W 1 start clap pattern together on ct 1 of meas 2.

IV

1—8   Two couples join R hands to make a star and move cw with 8 step-hops (M L, W L).

9—16   Reverse to L-hand star and move ccw with 8 step-hops.

V

1—16   M 2 and W 1 start clap pattern with each other on ct 1 of meas 1. M 1 and W 2 start clap pattern on ct 1 of meas 2.

VI

1—16   Take partner and waltz anywhere. Or form large circle and step-hop to L, then reverse. End dance with
hands raised.

Hints for Learning

Experiment with the clap pattern until the group feels at ease
with the rhythm. Notice that the dance has a staggered
rhythm pattern for couples, the second couple waiting until
the second measure to start clapping. When clapping the
thighs with both hands, bend your knees slightly. Some dancers find it helps to count, "Me, me, me, you, you, you"
during the clapping.

MISIRLOU

Misirlou, based on the Greek Kritikos, was originated by Greek-Americans. It has many variations and has found great popularity in America.

Nationality: Greek-American.
Record: Standard 5-131A.
Meter: 4/4.
Steps: Grapevine, two-step.
Formation: Single broken circle with hands joined at shoulder height.

Pattern in Brief
1. Step R, point L.
2. Grapevine R.
3. Two-step fwd cw.
4. Two-step bwd ccw.

Repeat entire dance.

Pattern

Meas

1–2   Introduction, no movement.
1   Step R ft R (ct 1, 2), point L toe fwd (ct 3), swing L ft around behind R ft (ct 4).
2   Step L behind R ft, step R to R side, step L in front of R (resembles a grapevine and body turns with foot movement). On ct 4 body pivots from facing ccw to cw. (Count: Step L, R, L, pivot L.)
3   Facing cw take 1 two-step starting with R ft. On ct 4 lift L ft to beside knee.
4   Without turning body, take 1 two-step backward, starting with L ft. On ct 4 turn to face front (R).

Repeat entire dance.

Hints for Learning
Practice the sequence of a two-step fwd starting with R ft and a two-step bwd starting with L ft. Work to turn the body naturally to follow the pattern of the feet. On the step and point, the body faces center of circle. On the grapevine, face cw, then center, then ccw. On the two-step, pivot to face cw.

LECH LAMIDBAR

Israeli dancing is termed folk dance, but, instead of being handed down through the years, our Israeli dances are products of a new and independent country. Dances included in this book are being danced today in Israel.

Pronunciation: Lekh lah-mid-bar.
Nationality: Israeli.
Record: Israel 118.
Meter: 4/4.
Steps: Leap, step-close, grapevine (cherkassiya).
Formation: Single circle facing center. Hands are joined and down.

Pattern in Brief
1. Leap R, cross, step, touch; side, together, side, touch.
2. Jump, kick, jump, kick; grapevine.
3. Step-touch R, step-touch L; fwd, close, back, close.
4. Grapevine with jump and turn to reverse LOD.

Pattern

Meas

I

1	During step always face center of circle. Leap to R onto R ft, cross L in front of R, step R to R, touch L to R.
2	Step L to L, close R to L, step L to L, touch R by L ft.
3—8	Repeat meas 1—2 three times.

II

1	Jump onto both ft, kick L fwd, jump both ft, kick R fwd.
2	Grapevine (cherkassiya)—cross R over L, step L to side, R behind L, step to side with L.
3—8	Repeat meas 1—2 three times.

III

1	Step R, touch L to side of R; step L, touch R to side of L.

2   Step fwd on R, at same time swinging arms fwd to shoulder level, close L to R; step bwd on R, close L to R and lower arms to sides.

3—4   Repeat meas 1—2.

IV

5—6   Grapevine moving to L: cross R ft over L (ct 1), step L to L (ct 2), cross R behind L (ct 3), step L to L (ct 4), cross R in front of L (ct 5), step L to L (ct 6), jump with weight on both ft twisting body ½ turn L (ct 7), leap onto R to face ccw kicking L heel up behind (ct 8).

7—8   Repeat meas 5—6 beginning on L ft and traveling to R.

9—12   Repeat meas 5—8 once.

Repeat entire dance.

Hints for Learning

The dance pattern moves to the R on step 1, to the L on step 2, to the R on step 3, and to the L on step 4. On the last grapevine, as you leap onto the L ft (cts 7—8), be sure to end facing the center of the circle so you are ready to start the dance over by leaping R to R.

VAYIVEN UZIYAHU

This was originally an all-men's dance composed to celebrate the Israeli Independence in 1956, and the vigorous quality of the dance is exemplified in the music. The dance was choreographed by Rivkah Sturman.

Pronunciation: Vah-yee-ven Oo-zee-*yah*-oo.
Nationality: Israeli.
Record: Festival-Symphony FS 201 LP.
Meter: 2/4.
Steps: Walk, run, bounce, leap, jump.
Formation: Single circle facing ccw, hands joined and held low.

Pattern in Brief
1. Starting on R ft: 4 runs, 4 bounces; 2 runs, 2 bounces; 2 runs, 2 bounces. Repeat.
2. Fwd 2, shoulder fwd and pull back. Repeat. Walk, walk (clap on walks), run, run, leap, leap. Jump, leap L, jump, leap L. Repeat sequence.

57

Repeat entire dance.

Pattern

Meas

1—4   Introduction, no movement.

I

1—2   Moving ccw, run 4 steps fwd beginning with R ft.
3—4   Face center of circle and with feet together bounce 4 times, lifting heels off floor but keeping balls of ft on floor.
5—6   Run ccw 2 steps, bounce twice facing center.
7—8   Run 2, bounce 2.
9—16   Repeat meas 1—8 (run 4, bounce 4, run 2, bounce 2, run 2, bounce 2).

II

1   Walk ccw R, L.
2   Stamp R fwd with R shoulder swinging fwd directly over R knee (ct 1), pull R shoulder back while shifting weight back to L ft (ct 2).
3—4   Repeat meas 1—2.
5   Walk fwd R, L. Clap hands on each step (this is only time you let go of hands).
6   Run fwd ccw two steps (R, L).
7   Leap fwd twice (R, L).
8   Jump on both ft facing directly to center of circle (ct 1). Leap onto L ft as you cross it in front of R (ct 2).
9   Jump again on both ft and leap onto L ft as you cross it in front of R. The body twists with this movement as the leap is high.
10—18   Repeat meas 1—9.

Repeat entire dance.

Hints for Learning
Because Vayiven Uziyahu includes many of the basic step patterns in folk dancing—the basic run, leap, jump, bounce, and walk—it is a good one to practice. The movements are strong and masculine.

MAYIM, MAYIM

Mayim, Mayim, which means "water, water," is danced the world over, according to a statement made by Rickey Holden after his tour around the world. The dance depicts the significance of water in the dry land of Israel.

Pronunciation: Ma-yeem.
Nationality: Israeli.
Record: Folkraft 1108A.
Meter: 4/4.
Steps: Grapevine, run, tap-step.
Formation: Single closed circle facing center, hands joined and held low.

Pattern in Brief
1. Grapevine.
2. Begin R, move to center with 4 runs, back out 4. Repeat.
3. Move cw 4 runs, face center on ct 4.
4. Tape toe and clap.

Repeat entire dance.

Pattern

Meas
1   Introduction, no movement.

I (*Grapevine*)

1—4   Facing center, cross R ft over L, step L to L, cross R ft behind L, leap L with L ft. Repeat three more times.
5   Run to center of circle with R, L, R, L, raising arms gradually above shoulder height.
6   Run 4 steps back to place starting with R ft and gradually lower arms to starting position.
7—8   Repeat meas 5—6.

II

1   Face cw, take 4 running steps starting with R ft.
2—3   Leap to R ft and extend L toe directly fwd to tap floor, hop R and extend L toe to L side.
         Repeat tap-step three more times.

59

4—5   Leap to L ft and extend R toe directly fwd to tap floor (clapping hands at same time in front of body, chest high), hop L and tap R toe to R, extending arms out to sides. Repeat three more times (clap hands when R toe taps in front of body).

Repeat entire dance.

Hints for Learning

The main thing to remember in fixing the pattern of this dance in your mind is that you start with the R ft in both figures. In the first figure you move toward the L by crossing R over L.

KOROBUSHKA

Korobushka, or "little basket," tells the story of a peddler who describes the numerous articles in his basket.

Pronunciation: Kor-ob-*oosh*-kah.
Nationality: Russian.
Record: Folk Dancer MH1059.
Meter: 2/4.
Steps: Schottische, Bokazo, balance step, three-step turn.
Formation: Double circle of partners facing and holding both hands. M in center.

Pattern in Brief
1. Schottische out, in, out, and Bokazo.
2. Turn R, turn L, balance and change places with partner. Turn R, turn L in place, balance with a new partner, change places.

Repeat entire dance with new partner.

> *Bokazo:* Hop L as you point R toe fwd in front of L toe (ct 1), hop L and place R ft pigeontoed by L ft (ct 2), slide heels together (ct 1), hold (ct 2). (W do same as M but hop on R ft and use L toe to point front, side, and click heels.)

Pattern

Meas

I

1—2   Starting with L ft (W R), take one schottische step fwd (W backs up).
3—4   Repeat meas 1—2 with M backing up to center of circle (W moves fwd).
5—6   Repeat meas 1—2.
7—8   Bokazo.

II

9—10   Hands on waist, M and W start with R ft and make three-step turn to own R. Step R, L, R, as you make full R turn. On ct 2 of meas 2 clap hands.

11—12 Repeat meas 9—10, starting with L ft and turning L.

13—14 Take partner's R hand, balance fwd with R ft, bwd L.

15—16 Change places with partner in 4 walking steps by arching W (L turn) under M's R arm. End facing partner.

17—18 Repeat meas 9—10 (three-step R turn).

19—20 Repeat action of meas 11—12, but instead of moving L with turn, turn L in place. This puts you in front of new partner.

21—24 Repeat meas 13—16 (balance and arch new W under R arm to return to starting position).

Repeat entire dance with new partner.

Hints for Learning

Practice the Bokazo in a single circle with the M starting on the L ft and pointing the R, W starting on the R ft and pointing the L. Both M and W start turn with the R ft while practicing in a single circle.

LOWLAND SCHOTTISCHE

Nationality: Scandinavian.
Record: Folk Dancer MH2003A.
Meter: 4/4.
Step: Schottische.
Formation: Double circle of partners, varsouvienne position, facing ccw. W on R.

Pattern in Brief
1. Basic schottische sequences fwd. Repeat.
2. W turns. Repeat.
3. Chase. Repeat.
4. W whirl across in front of M. Repeat.
5. Back-skaters' position and turn. Repeat.
6. M kneels, W dances around him. Repeat.
7. Diamond. Repeat.

Repeat entire dance.

Pattern

Meas

1—2   Introduction, no movement.

I

1—4   One basic schottische sequence (1-2-3 hop, 1-2-3 hop, 4 step-hops) fwd (ccw) in varsouvienne position—M L ft, W R ft.

5—8   Repeat meas 1—4. On step-hops, partners retain R-hand hold and W moves in front of M. M face ccw, W face cw.

II

9—16   Holding R hands, W in front of M, do 2 schottische sequences fwd (W bwd) with W turning R under M's raised R arm on step-hops.

III

1—2   *Chase:* L shoulders together, hands held down at side. W backs up diagonally toward wall, M moves diagonally fwd toward wall; reverse. One schottische fwd, turn, (R shoulders together, turn in toward

63

partner, hold R hands), and one schottische toward center of circle.

3—4   Turn alone on step-hops (R turn in circle).

5—8   Repeat meas 1—4.

IV

9—12   W on M's R side, W's L hand on M's R shoulder, M's R arm around partner's waist. Fwd with basic step, W whirls across to L side of M on first 2 step-hops and returns to M's R side on next 2.

13—16   Repeat meas 9—12.

V

1—4   *Back-skaters' position*: Join hands with partner behind backs (R to R, L to L, M's R arm on top). Move fwd with basic step, turn away from partner and reverse LOD on step-hops (do not let go of hands).

5—8   Repeat meas 1—4, moving RLOD.

VI

9—12   Hold inside hands and move fwd on basic step. M kneels, W dances around him on step-hops, making a full circle.

13—16   Repeat meas 9—12.

VII

1—4   *Diamond*: Partners move diagonally away from each other on first 1-2-3 hop, then partners move diagonally fwd toward each other on next 1-2-3 hop. Meet partner and take shoulder-waist position, turn R on step-hops.

5—8   Repeat meas 1—4.

Repeat entire dance.

Hints for Learning

The sequence is most easily learned from the arm positions. First, move through arm positions to see how naturally they follow each other: (1) varsouvienne; (2) with R hand lead W in front of M; (3) L shoulders together, hold L hands (M face wall, W face center of circle); (4) W's L hand on M's R shoulder; (5) drop hands behind back for back-skaters' position; (6) pull away slightly from partner to hold inside hands; (7) diamond.

ZIOGELIS

"The Grasshopper," as most dancers know this dance, is another introduced in this country by Vyts Beliajus. This, like so many Lithuanian dances, is an occupational dance telling a harvest story. The two-step portrays the romancing of the grasshoppers as they move through the rye.

Pronunciation: Zhyo-*gya*-liss.
Nationality: Lithuanian.
Record: Folkraft LP 35 ("Viltis").
Meter: 2/4.
Steps: Grasshopper, two-step, two-step balance.
Formation: Two sets of 3 people facing each other, M in center with arms around waists of W on each side. W's inside hands on M's shoulders.

Pattern in Brief
Chorus (grasshopper step).
1. Elbow swing and change sides. Chorus.
2. W slide across. Chorus.
3. Arches: M to R side, W arch across and back. Chorus.
4. Trio arch: R hand high, LW under. Chorus.
5. Circle 3, L and R. Chorus.
6. Circle 6, L and R.

Grasshopper step: All start with R ft, dance fwd with 2 two-steps. Finish second by bending L knee in fwd dip. Starting with R ft, do 2 two-steps bwd, ending with bwd dip. As you dip fwd, body leans fwd. As you dip bwd, body leans back. Repeat meas 1—8.

Pattern

Meas

1—2 Introduction, no movement.

I

1—8 Chorus (grasshopper step).
9—12 W on M's R move into center, hooking R elbows to turn one and one-half times and change sides. This takes 4 two-steps. W on M's L and M do two-step balance in place (step R, ball change, step L, ball change).
13—16 Repeat meas 9—12, with W on M's L changing sides.

II

1—8 Chorus (grasshopper step).
9—12 W on M's R face M, slide back to original position, passing opposite W back to back. M and L W two-step balance.
13—16 Repeat meas 9—12, with L W sliding to original place.

III

1—8 Chorus (grasshopper step).
9—16 M slide in front of R W 4 slides, two-step balance for 4, then slide back to place in 4 slides. At same time W join hands (inside) and change sides, with W in set # 1 making arch as W in set # 2 dive under arch.

67

Turn in toward partner and two-step back to place with W in set # 2 making arch.

IV

1—8   Chorus (grasshopper step).

9—12   4 two-steps. M makes arch with R hand high; L W goes under as W cross in front of M. M follows L W under arch and set faces out.

13—16 Repeat meas 9—12, with L hand high and R W under; M follows R W and set faces center again.

V

1—8   Chorus (grasshopper step).

9—12   Join hands in circles of 3 and move cw with 4 two-steps.

13—16 Reverse circles of 3 and move ccw with 4 two-steps.

VI

1—8   Chorus (grasshopper step).

9—16   Join hands in circle of 6, moving cw with 4 two-steps. Reverse for 3 two-steps and end by swinging arms fwd and up and calling HEY.

Hints for Learning

This dance can be memorized in pairs. In the first two figures, the ladies change sides. The next two figures are arch figures. The last two are circles.

RAKSI JAAK

This threesome dance can be done with either one man and two women, or three women, or one woman and two men forming a set.

Pronunciation: Rahk-see yak.
Nationality: Estonian.
Record: Folk Dancer MH3007B.
Meter: 2/4.
Steps: Walk, polka.
Formation: Sets of 3, all facing center of hall, hands joined at shoulder height.

Pattern in Brief
1. Chorus.
2. Arch figure, R hand high. L W under. Chorus.
3. W back up, M fwd (triangle), reverse, W turning. Chorus.
4. Cuddle position, polka fwd, polka bwd, and W turn to original position. Chorus.

Repeat entire dance.

Pattern

Meas

1—2	Introduction, no movement.

Chorus

1	All step L to L, touch R beside L.
2	All step R to R, touch L beside R.
3—4	Repeat meas 1—2.
5—6	Walk fwd 3 steps (L, R, L), kick R ft fwd.
7—8	Walk bwd 4 steps (R, L, R, L).

I

9—16	M polkas in place. Both W polka around M retaining hand hold. As W cross in front, R W arches over as L W goes under arch. W cross in back, L W arching high as R W goes under. Keep hands high, as M faces front during arches.
1—8	Chorus. On last meas, W turn in to face M, forming

triangle. W's backs to center, M face center.

II

9—12   Polka 4 steps toward center of circle, W pulling M.
13—16   Reverse direction, W release hands and turn toward M and under his arms for 4 polka steps.

1—8   Chorus. On last meas, W turn in toward M to cuddle position (L W makes R turn, R W makes L turn. M has arms around W's waists).

III

9—12   Dance 4 polka steps fwd.
13—14   Dance 2 polka steps bwd.
15—16   W turn out to original positions with 2 polka steps.

Repeat entire dance.

Hints for Learning

When practicing this dance, the group should face the front of the room so that all dancers are moving in the same direction. The Estonian polka is done without lifting the feet far off the floor.

OSLO WALTZ

Michael and Mary Ann Herman introduced this old-time Scotch-English waltz to the United States where it has become known as the "good-night" waltz. It is used often as the final number on a program, because it gives friends an opportunity to bid farewell.

Nationality: Scotch-English.
Record: Folk Dancer MH3016.
Meter: 3/4.
Steps: Waltz, waltz balance.
Formation: Single circle of couples facing center, W on R.

Pattern in Brief
1. Waltz balance as W moves ccw around circle.
2. Waltz balance toward center and turn, then toward wall and turn.
3. Step-draw.
4. Waltz turn in ballroom position.

Repeat entire dance.

Waltz Balance: Step fwd L, step-close R to L, step L in place. Repeat with M stepping bwd on R ft.
Step-draw: Step L ft to L, bring R ft to instep of L ft (you slide R ft on floor using the ball of the foot).

Pattern

Meas

1—8   Introduction, no movement.

I

1—2   Waltz balance fwd and back, W begin with R ft, M with L.
3—4   With 2 waltz steps in place, M takes W on L side and brings her across in front of him to R side, changing hands. W takes 2 waltz steps as she turns R a full turn toward M while changing sides, and ends facing center of circle.
5—16   Repeat waltz balance and crossover three times. On

fourth cross over, W faces fourth M and takes closed dance position, M facing LOD.

II

1—2 Ballroom position, balance toward center and away from center, M begin with L ft, W with R.

3—4 Turn away from partner, one full turn. M turn L and W turn R with 1 waltz step and 2 walks.

5—8 Repeat meas 1—4, balancing away from center of circle, then toward center. End with M turning R and W turning L with one waltz step and 2 walks.

9—12 Join hands with partner, elongated hold, shoulder height. M begin with L ft, W with R, take 2 step-draws toward center of circle, then 2 step-draws away from center.

13—16 In ballroom dance position, take 4 turning waltz steps, moving ccw, turning cw. On fourth waltz step, open up to single circle.

Repeat entire dance.

Hints for Learning

The American waltz is often confused with our popular two-step. When waltzing, you should be aware of the foot closing on ct 3, rather than on ct 2 as in the two-step. The Landler waltz—used in many of our European dances—uses a down-up-up, or flat-toe-toe motion, while the American waltz moves fwd, side, close.

POD BOREM

Pod Borem is a simple but typical dance that is a form of the popular Polish Krakowiak, which was popular with the peasants of Krakow.

Nationality: Polish.
Record: Bruno NR 50017 Side A Band 2.
Meter: 4/4.
Steps: Pas de basque, walk, clicks.
Formation: Double circle, couples facing, M back to center. Inside hands joined and held shoulder height, outside hands on waist, fingers fwd.

Pattern in Brief
1. Pas de basque.
2. Walk & click.

Pattern

Meas

1—3   Introduction, no movement.

I

1—3   6 pas de basque. M start L and W R. There is a slight feeling of back to back and face to face.

II

4   M start L, W start R, walk 3 steps in LOD; swing arms fwd on ct 3, end back to back, click free ft (M R, W L).

5   Walk 3 steps in LOD (M R, W L); swing arms bwd on ct 3, end facing, click free foot (M L, W R).

6—7   Repeat meas 4—5; join both hands, elongated hold.

8   4 continuous clicks starting with weight on M R, W L. Move in LOD.

Repeat entire dance.

Hints for Learning
Imagine a small log or a narrow ditch of water. As you practice the pas de basque, jump over the log or ditch and remem-

ber that when you move right, you start with the R ft; when you move L, start with the L ft. Count: leap, ball change or leap right, ball change, leap left, ball change.

SAUERLANDER QUADRILLE

This is one of the many German dances Paul and Gretel Dunsing have presented to the folk dance world. Sauerlander Quadrille is from Neheim-Husten, and the basic step pattern, the Neheimer step, is taken from the name of the village.

Nationality: German.
Record: Folk Dancer MH1120.
Meter: 4/4.
Step: Neheimer step (N.S.)
Formation: Four couples in a square numbered 1-3-2-4, ccw, couple # 1 with back to music, W on R.

Pattern in Brief
1. Peek-a-boo, 1-2-3-4.
2. Couples to R and back, 1-2-3-4.
3. Couples cross over: 1 & 2, then 3 & 4; 1 & 2 back, then 3 & 4 back.
4. R-hand star, 1-2-3-4.
5. Grand Slam (all 4 couples); 1 & 2 cross over as 3 & 4 peek-a-boo; 3 & 4 cross over as 1 & 2 peek-a-boo. Repeat. All 4 couples to R and back, all four R-hand star. Repeat.

Neheimer Step:
1. Dancing in place: hop on L ft, put R toe (knee turned in) by ball of L ft (ct 1), hop on L ft, touch R toe by ball of L ft (swing R knee out) (ct 2); hop on L ft, touch R heel straight fwd (ct 3), hop on L ft, touch R toe by ball of L ft (ct 4).

2. Moving to side: step R to R side, step L behind R, bring both feet together and bounce twice on toes.

3. Dancing in place: repeat meas 1 by hopping on R ft and touching L toe.

4. Moving to side: step L, R behind L, and with slight jump land on both feet (ct 3) to finish step. Double bounce is used when step continues; if step is finished, you use single jump and hold ct 4.

Moving fwd: when using N.S. to move fwd, use following count: Toe, toe, heel, toe, fwd, fwd, bounce,

bounce. Toe, toe, heel, toe, fwd, fwd; twist in toward partner with single jump to face center of set.

Pattern

Meas

1—4   Introduction. Hold meas 1—2, honor partner on meas 3, honor corner on meas 4.

I

1—4   *Peek-a-boo*: M 1 and opposite W 2 dance one N.S. to corner of square, (M L, W R) look at each other behind couple 4, return to place with 1 N.S. (M R, W L).

5—16   Couples take turns with meas 1—4. M 2 and W 1 look around couple 3, M 3 and W 4 look around couple 1, then M 4 and W 3 look around couple 2.

II

1—4   *To R and back*: Couple 1 face each other and do 1 N.S. to own R (begin R ft) and 1 N.S. back to place (W to center and M to outside of set).

5—16   Couples take turns, with 2, 3, and 4 repeating to R and back.

III

1—4   *Crossover*: Couples 1 and 2 move toward each other with 1 N.S. (begin R ft). Meet in straight line with R shoulders to opposite person (M on outside). Continue to opposite side with 1 N.S. and, on jump, turn in toward partner to face center of set.

5—8   Couples 3 and 4 do action of meas 1—4.

9—16   Repeat meas 1—8 to return to original places. Couples 1 and 2, then 3 and 4. Pass R shoulders with opposite both times, so that on return, W are on outside.

IV

1—4   *R-hand star*: Couple 1 face, hold R hands. Start with L ft and do 1 N.S. to change places. Repeat, starting with R ft to return to starting place.

5—16   Couples take turns with R-hand star; 2, 3, then 4.

V

1—4   *Grand Slam*: All 4 couples work together for remainder of dance. Couples 1 and 2 cross over as 3 and 4 do peek-a-boo step.

5—8   Couples 3 and 4 cross over as 1 and 2 do peek-a-boo.

9—16   Repeat meas 1—8, with all couples returning to original place.

17—20   All 4 couples to R and back.

21—24   All 4 couples R-hand star.

25—32   Repeat meas 17—24.

Hints for Learning

This dance has a suspense that gives it an element of comedy. No one knows who is going to perform next, and dancers do not move into dance position until ct 1 of step. A dancer remains facing the center of the square until it is his turn to dance, then he turns quickly into the Neheimer step. As he finishes the step, he always faces the center of the set again. When dancing, keep arms at the side of the body, stand tall, and make the step patterns sharp but not exaggerated.

CZARDAS VENGERKA

The very popular Czardas from Hungary has many variations. Andor Czompo introduced this favorite couple dance.

Pronunciation: Char-dah-sh Veng-er-kah.
Nationality: Hungarian.
Record: RCA Victor EPA 4126.
Meter: 4/4.
Steps: Step-close, Bokazo, reel, walk.
Formation: Couples in double circle.

Pattern in Brief
1. Step-close and Bokazo.
2. Reel, walk, turn.

Repeat entire dance.

Pattern

Meas

I

1   Moving diagonally fwd to R, step R, close L to R, step fwd R, close L to R.
2   *Bokazo:* M & W—Hop L, pt R toe fwd, heel slightly turned in (ct 1). Hop on L ft and pt R toe to side, heels of both feet slightly turned out (ct 2); with sharp clicking movement close R heel to L heel (ct 3) and hold (ct 4).
3—4 Repeat meas 1—2 moving diagonally fwd L.
5—8 Repeat meas 1—4.

II

1   Partners face, M back to center. Starting R, take 4 reel steps (skip back), moving away from partner.
2   Bokazo.
3   Make a complete R turn with 4 walking steps; finish facing partner.
4   Bokazo.
5   Moving toward partner step R, step L, stamp R, L, touch R.

6   Bokazo.
7   With 4 walking steps, start R ft and make individual
       turn cw. End standing by partner facing ccw.
8   Bokazo.

       Repeat entire dance.

Hints for Learning

Practice the Bokazo starting with the hop on the L ft. Then
start the Bokazo hopping on the R ft. The styling is smooth
with a proud carriage of the body.

SALTY DOG RAG

A popular American round dance that has excitement and fast movement. An excellent dance to be used in parade routes where progressive movement is needed. A crowd pleaser for European audiences.

Nationality: American.
Record: Decca 27981.
Meter: 4/4.
Steps: Schottische. (All patterns start on R ft.)
Formation: Promenade position, R hands on top, moving ccw.

Pattern in Brief
1. Grapevine schottische fwd.
2. Cross over.
3. Heel step. (Advanced version uses pivot turn and step-brush.

Repeat entire dance.

Pattern

Meas

1—8	Introduction, no movement.

I

1—2	Both start with R ft. Take 2 schottische steps moving diagonally R then diagonally L; step diagonally R, L behind, R to side.
3—4	Four step-hops starting with R ft (move forward ccw).
5—8	Repeat 1—4.

II

1—2	Drop R hands retaining L-hand hold, change places with one schottische step, W going in front of M toward LOD. Using slight resistance against L hand of partner to start turn, whirl into individual full L turn, returning to original place using one schottische step.
3—4	Grasp R hands shoulder height and with 4 step-hops

       make complete circle cw bringing W back to outside of circle.

5—8   Repeat 1—4 grasping L hands for initial cross over.

III

1—2   Place R heel fwd, step on R ft in place, place L heel fwd, step on L ft, place feet in pigeon-toe position, then bring heels together, stamp R, stamp L.

3—4   Four step-hops fwd, R, L, R, L.

5—8   Repeat 1—4.

ADVANCED VERSION FOR III
(To be used in place of original III)

1—2   Holding R hands, W slightly in front of M, W make R pivot turn (complete turn on R ft, step fwd on L). Repeat 2 times then stamp R, L. M step R, brush L fwd, step L, brush R fwd, step R, brush L fwd, stamp L, touch R with no weight on R ft.

3—4   Take promenade position and move ccw 4 step-hops, starting R ft.

5—8   Repeat 1—4.

Repeat entire dance.

Hints for Learning

On step II the W crosses over in front of the M and returns in the same line pattern. If the dancer has difficulty with a grapevine schottische, a schottische fwd may be substituted.

HAMBO

Recognized as the national dance of Sweden, the Hambo is a favorite dance of all the Scandinavian countries.

Pronunciation: Hahm-bo.
Nationality: Swedish.
Record: MH2003A.
Meter: 3/4.
Steps: Waltz, hambo turn.
Formation: Couples anywhere on floor, facing LOD. Hold inside hands in open position.

Pattern in Brief
1. Waltz.
2. Hambo turn. (W and M are using different step patterns. M stamp R, step L, touch R; W step L, touch R, step R.)

Repeat entire dance.

Pattern

Meas

I

1—3	M L, W R, move forward LOD with 3 waltz steps (Landler waltz step with slight dip on ct 1, walking fwd on ct 2—3).
4	M stamps R as he turns inward toward partner, taking closed dance position. W steps L, moving into closed position (ct 1). M steps L in sideward movement as W touches R toe behind L ft (ct 2). On ct 3 M touches R toe on floor beside L ft, W steps R.
5—7	Continue hambo turn, closed position, 3 times.
8	End facing LOD and walk fwd 3 steps, joining inside hands.

Repeat entire dance.

Hints for Learning

The group separates so that the M are working separately from the W. Moving fwd, without the turn, the M practice 3 waltz steps forward and then count, R, L, touch R toe (repeat 3 times), walk fwd 3 steps. Move then into the hambo turn, working independently of a partner. Then the partners work together. W use this same procedure. As the group dances with partners, the directions are called for the M for a sequence, then for the W. Change partners often to make learning faster. There are two variations to styling: (1) very smooth and gliding; (2) an accented dip on the first step of the turn.

Weathervane

King's Cross

KREUZ KOENIG

The patterns of the dance resemble the King's Cross. The music is a classic, for it has definite breaks in the musical pattern to accompany the changes in the dance patterns.

Pronunciation: Kroyts Kenig.
Nationality: German.
Record: Folk Dancer MH1052.
Meter: 3/4.
Steps: Leap, run, step-hop, mazurka.
Formation: 2 couples in circle, hands joined, W on R.

Pattern in Brief
1. Circle 4.
2. Weathervane—M cross L elbows.
3. Figure 8.
4. Mazurka—circle 4, then circle with partner.
5. King's Cross with W back to back.

Repeat entire dance.

Pattern

Meas

1—2   Introduction, no movement.
3—4   Bow to partner.

I

1—2   *Circle four*: Moving cw, leap onto L, cross R behind L, step L, turn to face cw and take 3 running steps fwd (R, L, R).
3—8   Repeat meas 1—2 three times.

II

1—8   *Weathervane*: Release hand hold, M puts R arm around partner's waist (make sure M's R arm is under W's L arm), and M cross L arms at elbows, reaching behind other M to clasp opposite W's hand. M's L hand and opposite W's L hand are joined behind her partner's back. All run fwd ccw 24 steps.

85

III

1–2   *Figure 8*: M release hands so that couples face each other in single line, W at ends. W take 2 step-hops in place as M take L hands and exchange places in 2 step-hops.

3–4   M takes R hand of opposite W and step-hops around her, turning her in 2 step-hops.

5–6   W take 2 step-hops in place as M take L hands and exchange places in 2 step-hops.

7–8   M takes R hand of partner and turns her around in 2 step-hops, completing the full figure 8 pattern.

9–16   Repeat meas 1–8.

IV

1   *Mazurka*: Join hands in circle of 4, W on M's R. Moving cw step L ft diagonally fwd, bring R ft to L with cut step, hop on R ft and bring L ft across R leg in sweeping movement. (This is 1 mazurka step.)

2–4   Repeat meas 1 three times.

5–6   M release opposite W's hand and join hands with partner, and move cw in small circle with 2 mazurka steps.

7–8   Bring arms to shoulder height; both M and W extend R arm across partner's chest and bend L elbow. With hands still joined, take 6 running steps moving cw.

9–16   Repeat meas 1–8. At the end of 6 running steps, M shake R hands with partners, placing W back to back, and join L hands with opposite W.

V

1–3   *King's Cross*: M, facing slightly to L, take 8 running steps fwd moving cw. W, acting as pivot point, run in place with slight kick fwd.

4   During next 4 running steps, M release W's L hands and pull with their R, exchanging places with W.

5–8   Repeat meas 1–4 with M back to back in center.

9–16   Repeat meas 1–8.

Repeat entire dance.

Hints for Learning

Use the single circle to practice the step patterns. Two important things to remember about this dance: During the weathervane, all hands are behind backs. During the King's Cross figure, partners never release R hands.

Circle Four

Buzz Step

HOPAK

The Hopak is the national dance of the Ukrainian people and one of the most exciting challenges for the dancer. Every step used in this dance can be found in numerous Ukrainian and Russian dances.

Pronunciation: Ho-pahk.
Nationality: Ukrainian.
Record: Kismet 106.
Meter: 4/4.
Steps: Pas de basque, Russian polka, buzz-step turn, prysiadkas, lunge step, touch-kick, toe-heel-cross-kick.
Formation: Double circle facing LOD, men on inside, partners in varsouvienne position. A variation on starting is to take varsouvienne position but M place R hands on W's waists, W hold beads with L hands.

Pattern in Brief
 1. Pas de basque.
 2. Touch, kick, run-2-3.
 3. Russian polka.
 4. Buzz-step turns alone.
 5. Lunge steps—lunge fwd L, cut R, run-2-3.
 6. Buzz-step turns with partner.
 7. Push steps to R, L, R, then L.
 8. Toe-heel-cross-kick steps.
 9. M prysiadka, W pas de basque.
10. Buzz-step turns with partner. End with diagonal turn.

Pattern

Meas

I

1—16 Couples pas de basque in varsouvienne position, facing ccw. M & W start on R ft. (The majority of Ukrainian dances start on R ft.)

II

1—4 Touch, kick, run-2-3 (touch R ft in front of L shin, extend R ft with toe at mid-calf, run fwd R, L, R). Repeat, touching L ft in front of R shin.

5—16 Repeat meas 1—4 three times.

III

1—16 16 Russian polka steps (Leap fwd on R, run fwd L, R, leap fwd on L, run fwd R, L.) Count: Leap, run, run.) Keep feet lifts very close to floor and make movement smooth.

IV

1—16 Buzz-step turn alone (2 buzz steps per meas). All turn R with 15 buzz steps, then on 16 clap hands while reversing direction. Take 15 buzz steps turning to L, clap hands on 16; end facing ccw.

V

1—4 Take partner in varsouvienne position and lunge fwd onto R ft bending R knee (keep body erect), then bring L ft fwd and cut-step (change weight to L ft and extend R ft fwd). Step fwd R, L, R. Repeat,

89

lunging fwd onto L ft.

5—16   Repeat meas 1—4 three times.

VI

1—16   Buzz-step turn with partner. Outside arm is held high with slight arch, arm nearest partner is around his or her waist. R hips together for 15 buzz steps, on 16 clap and reverse to L hips together. Repeat buzz-step turn for 15, then clap and end facing each other, W face LOD, M face reverse LOD.

VII

1—8   Push to own R away from partner for 8 push steps and return with 8 push steps, clapping while changing direction. W move out of circle, M into circle.

9—16   Repeat meas 1—8.

VIII

1—16   Toe-heel-cross-kick; partners facing, W ccw, M cw (both start R ft). M lift both arms to ceiling. When kicking R, kick diagonally to own R so that you won't hit partner.

IX

1—16   M prysiadka (deep-knee squats, coffee grinders, aerial splits—see Glossary) in center of circle as W face center and do 16 pas de basque, leap to R.

X

1—16   Buzz-step turn with partner, R hips together for 15 buzz-steps, on 16 clap and reverse to L hips together. Buzz-step for 12; on 13—14 M and W join R hands, M turn W in full L turn. On 15—16 grasp L hands taking diagonal pull back with R arms arched.

Hints for Learning

First, practice each step pattern separately with music. To memorize the dance, learn the following story: (The first 3 steps are typical of Hopak dances, so memorize them.) On step 4 you turn alone. You are dizzy; so on step 5 you fall or lunge fwd. On step 6 you need someone to hold you up; so turn with your partner. Now you feel all right so put the W directly in front of you facing cw. You feel sprightly; so on 7 you push away. Last chance to get even with your partner (a stray kick does get into the dance); on 8 you do a toe-heel-cross-kick. M feel strong so on step 9 they do prysiadka. Step 10 is the happy ending as you turn together.

CORRIDO

A familiar folk ballad, "Corrido," provides the musical background for a dance that uses typical Mexican step patterns.

Nationality: Mexican.
Record: Selco 7420.
Meter: 4/4.
Steps: Step-close, grapevine, soldado.
Formation: Double circle of couples in conversation position, M's back to center.

Pattern in Brief

I

1. 10 step-close, moving cw.
2. Basic grapevine 7, on 8 cross & stamp.
3. 4 step-close and soldado (cut pie).
4. Basic grapevine 7, on 8 cross & stamp.

II

1. Repeat action of 1.
2. Cross-step with full turn.
3. Repeat action of 3.
4. M does continuous grapevine, W does grapevine with two turns.

III

1. Repeat action of 1.
2. Repeat action of 2, figure I.
3. Repeat action of 3, figure I.
4. Basic grapevine holding inside hands.

Pattern

Meas

I

(Steps described are for M; W use opposite footwork.)

1—5 M starting on R ft, W on L ft, take 10 step-close steps RLOD (step R, ct 1, bring L ft to R, ct &). When taking 10th step-close, be sure to put weight on L ft to free R ft for grapevine.

II

1—7   M start R, W start L. Take 7 basic grapevine steps ccw. (M cross R ft in front of L, step L to side, cross R ft behind L, step L ft to side, continue for total of 7 grapevine steps.)

8   M cross R ft over L, stamp L, R. W cross L over R, stamp R, L.

III

1—2   In closed position, M back to center, take 4 step-close steps RLOD.

3   *Soldado*: This figure represents the cutting of a piece of pie. M start with R ft, back into center with 4 walking steps.

4   M leads diagonally L out of center with 4 walking steps.

5—10   Repeat this figure three times. On third time coming out of center, M steps L, stamps R, L.

IV

1—8   Repeat action of figure II, meas 1—8 of basic grapevine. Repeat dance twice. Figures I and III remain same throughout entire dance.

SECOND TIME THROUGH DANCE

I

1—5   Repeat figure I of first sequence.

II

1   Face partner, M with hands held behind back, W holding skirt. M start with R ft, W with L. Step R across L taking weight on R and lifting L slightly, step L in place, step R at R side of L, cross L over R, lifting R ft slightly off ground.

2   Take 4-step turn, starting by stepping R behind L. M turn L, W turn R (ccw).

3—6   Repeat meas 1—2 twice.

7   Repeat meas 1.

8   Stamp R, L, R, hold to finish pattern.

III

1—10   Repeat figure III of first sequence.

IV

1—2   M do continuous grapevine step, moving ccw around circle. W do 1 meas of grapevine step, then during next measure do two pivot turns to R, arching under M's L arm.

3—8   Repeat meas 1—2 three times.

THIRD TIME THROUGH DANCE

Repeat first sequence, varying only grapevine of figure IV, thus: Holding inside hands only, do grapevine, swinging hands fwd as ft crosses in front, and swinging the hands back as ft crosses behind. End facing with L, R stamp, free hands lifted toward ceiling.

Hints for Learning

Corrido is repeated three times. Memorize the four patterns in the first sequence. Patterns I and III are always the same. The only basic changes come during the second time through the dance, when both grapevine figures have a turning step to remember.

SWEETS OF MAY

Sweets of May has all of the typical characteristics of an Irish dance. It comes from the northern part of Ireland and was introduced to dancers in the United States by Sean and Una O'Farrell.

Nationality: Irish.
Record: National N4514A.
Meter: 4/4.
Steps: 7s and 3s, skip change of step.
Formation: Four couples in square dance formation, numbered ccw.

Pattern in Brief
1. 7s and 3s to L and R, then to R and L. Chorus.
2. Promenade. Chorus.
3. Arches. Chorus.
4. Thread the needle.
5. 7s and 3s to L and R, then to R and L.

7s and 3s: Always step behind on ct 1. This step can be done moving to the L by stepping on the R ft on ct 1 as well as moving to the R by stepping on the L ft on ct 1. Weight on L ft, swing R back of L and step on R (ct 1), step L to L (ct 2), step R behind L (ct 3), step L to L (ct 4), step R behind L (ct 1), step L to L (ct 2), step R behind L (ct 3), hop on R (ct 4). Step L behind R (ct 1), step R in place (ct 2), step L in place (ct 3), hop on L (ct 4). Step R behind L (ct 1), step L in place (ct 2), step R in place (ct 3). This completes one 7's and 3's moving to the L. To move R, reverse the above step pattern.

Skip change of step: (Three in jig time.) Step fwd R (ct 1), close L to R heel (ct 2), step fwd R (ct 3), hop on R (ct 4). Step fwd L (ct 1), close R to L heel (ct 2), step fwd L (ct 3), hop on L (ct 4).

Pattern

Meas

1—8   Introduction, no movement.

I

1—4   Moving L, stepping with R ft behind L, do one 7's and 3's step.

5—8   Moving R back to place do another 7's and 3's step.

1—4   Move R with 7's and 3's step. Weight is on L ft at end of last 3's, so push off on R toe (ct &), step L behind R (ct 1) to start 7's and 3's.

5—8   Move L back to starting place with 7's and 3's step.

Chorus

1—2   Use skip change of step when moving; when standing in place dance 3's.
Couples 1 and 3 exchange places with 2 skip change of step. Hold inside hand; M will pass L shoulders in the center of square as they cross over.

3—4   Couples 1 and 3 turn in toward partner to reverse directions as couples 2 and 4 exchange places with 2 skip change of step.

5—6   Couples 1 and 3 return home, W pass L shoulders in the center of square. Couples 2 and 4 reverse direction.

7—8   Couples 2 and 4 return home. Couples 1 and 3 reverse direction.

9—10   Couples 1 and 3 fwd with 2 skip change of step and bow or curtsy.

11—12 Couples 2 and 4 repeat action of meas 9—10 as couples 1 and 3 back out with 2 skip change of step.

13—14 Couples 1 and 3 move fwd with 2 skip change of step as couples 2 and 4 back out with 2 skip change of step.

15—16 Couples 2 and 4 do 3's in place as couples 1 and 3 back up with 2 skip change of step.

17—18 All face center. Clap thighs twice, own hands twice, clap thighs twice, own hands twice.

19—20 Change places with partner, W passing in front of M, with 7's and 3's step. (M step L behind R to start 7's and 3's, W step R behind L).

21—24 Repeat claps and change places with partner. This time M passes in front of W.

II

1—16 *Promenade*: Partners facing ccw, hands joined, promenade around with 7 skip change of step. On 8 turn in toward partner to reverse LOD. Repeat promenade cw, ending in starting place, facing center on meas 8.

1—24 Chorus.

III

1—8 *Arches*: Couples 1 and 3 face couple on their R (1 faces 2, 3 faces 4). Head couples (1 & 3) arch over side couples for 2 skip change of step, changing places. Turn in toward partner for 2 skip change of step to reverse direction. Couples 2 and 4 arch high with couples 1 and 3 going under arch back to home. Turn in toward your partner for 2 skip change of step to end facing center.

9—16 Repeat arches, couples 1 and 3 facing couple on their L. Head couples always arch first.

1—24 Chorus.

IV

1—16 *Thread the needle*: Join hands in circle with break between M 1 and W 4. Couple 1 arches and W 4 leads line under arch, around in circle, and home (do not let go of hands). Couple 4 arches and M 1 leads line under arch and home (use skip change of step).

V

1—16 Repeat figure I (7s and 3s step in circle).

Hints for Learning

When doing the 7s and 3s, remember always to step behind on ct 1. Use five fingers to memorize the sequence of this dance. One and 5 are the same: 7's and 3's. The middle finger is the highest so it represents the arch figure. You have only 2 other figures to remember. Two represents the promenade and 4 represents threading the needle. Now, count the sequence using the finger method.

SHEPHERD'S CROOK

The Shepherd's Crook is a Scottish strathspey presented by Bruce McClure of Glasgow, Scotland. It is a very popular dance requiring one man and two ladies.

Nationality: Scottish.
Record: Parlophone PMD 1029, Side 2 band 2.
Meter: 4/4.
Steps: Strathspey traveling step, strathspey setting step, strathspey rocking step, Highland fling step.
Formation: Sets of 3, M between 2 W.

Pattern in Brief
1. Promenade.
2. Rocking step.
3. Shepherd's crook.
4. M schottische with each W.
5. Reel of three.
6. Highland fling step, rock on toe & heel, circle.
7. Highland fling step and turn.

Pattern

Meas

Introduction: chords. M bow fwd from waist, W curtsy. Turn R to face foot of hall. Join hands in lines of three.

I

1—4   *Promenade*: Four strathspey traveling steps toward foot of hall. Step fwd R, close L to R, step fwd R, lift R heel slightly as L ft swings through and reaches fwd for next step. Knees are turned out at all times. At end of meas 4 drop hands, all turn R toward head of hall.

5—8   Repeat 4 strathspey steps toward head of hall.

II

1—8   *Rocking step*: Four strathspey rocking steps. Beginning R, step fwd R, hop R, step back L, hop L; grapevine to L stepping R ft behind, L ft to side, R ft diagonally L in front and hop R. Step fwd L, hop L, back R, grapevine to R.

III

1—4   *Shepherd's crook*: M and W on left form arch for W 1 (on R) to go under and return to place using 4 strathspey steps. M & W 2 (on L) dance in place, and on meas 3 man follows W 1 under arch. On meas 4 W 2 turns R under her R arm. This entire movement is large.

5—8   Repeat with W 1 making arch for W 2. M follows under arch on meas 7; W 1 turns under her L arm on meas 8.

IV

Schottische: M dances with W 1 (on R side) as W 2 stands facing head of hall. The footwork is opposite for M & W.

1   M & W 1 in closed position. M pt L ft fwd, bring L toe behind calf, pt L ft fwd, bring L toe in front of calf while hopping on R ft.

2   Step to side with L, close R to L, hop on L as you extend R toe fwd touching floor, then touch back of calf with toe of R ft as you hop L at same time.

3—4   Repeat meas 1—2 with man beginning, pointing R ft fwd, W opposite. Move to M's R.

5—8   M and W 1 join hands in circle and dance 4 strathspey steps cw. M finishes in original position facing W 2.

9—16   Repeat 1—8 with W 2, moving toward foot of hall.

V

1—8   *Reel of three*: In line of 3, M and W 1 face; W 2 faces toward M. Starting with R ft all travel 8 strathspey steps, making figure 8. W 2 dances one step in place before becoming part of figure 8. Pass R shoulder first (in figure 8 always pass R shoulder on R side of 3's and L on L side of 3's).

VI

1   *Highland fling and rock step*: In line of 3 facing fwd, hop L, pt R to side, hop L, pt R behind calf, hop L, pt R to side, hop L, pt R in front of calf.

2   Put weight on ball of R ft directly in front of L ft as you touch L toe directly behind R ft. Rock back on ball of L ft, pt R toe directly in front of L. Repeat rock fwd on R, back on L.

3—8   Repeat meas 1—2 three times, alternating fling step & rock L, R, L (ct: side behind, side in front, rock 2, 3, 4).

VII

1   *Highland fling step:* Three Highland fling steps beginning with hop on L and pt R to side, hop L, pt R ft behind calf, hop L, pt R ft in front of calf, hop

2	Step on outside of poles on R side with R ft as far fwd as possible (ct 1), step back to back with partner inside poles L, R (ct 2, 3).
3	Reach with L as far back as you can while you leap L outside poles. Now facing partner, leap R, L between the poles.
4—15	Repeat meas 2—3 six times.
16	End with double hop R between poles, facing partner. This is transition to next step.

V

1	*Diagonal*: Hold R hand as you leap to L on L ft; leap R, L, between poles. On ct 3, change to L-hand hold.
2	Hold L hands as you leap to R on R ft; leap L, R, between poles. On ct 3 change to R-hand hold.
3—16	Repeat diagonal pullback fourteen times.

VI

1—16	*Feet apart*: Repeat figure III.

VII

1—16	*Chase*: Repeat figure II.

VIII

1—16	*Tinikling step*: Repeat figure I, but face partner and move in opposition to partner.

Note: On figures IV and V you can use a reverse pattern. This description makes the pattern easier for the two steps without using the variation.

Hints for Learning

All transitions and changes of LOD are done with a double hop between the poles. Sequence can be memorized by remembering that the dance goes 1—2—3, do-sa-do, diagonal pullback, 3—2—1. Tinikling is excellent as a challenge for coordination and skill. For a greater challenge, cross four poles. Even though the dance is usually done by couples, it can be used in groups of all women or all men.

Starting Position

MAORI STICK GAME

The Maori Stick Game is a favorite of the Maori people of New Zealand. Performed by the Kia Ora Club of Brigham Young University, and introduced to the classes by Dr. Leona Holbrook, this rhythm game appeals to all ages.

Nationality: New Zealand (Maori).
Record: Brigham Young University, Provo, Utah. Contact Dr. Leona Holbrook.
Meter: 3/4.
Steps: Single pass, double pass, in and out, flip, exchange, square, flourish.
Formation: Partners sitting opposite each other, about 3 ft apart.
Equipment: A pair of sticks for each player. Doweling 1 1/8" in diameter can be purchased at lumber yards in 15" lengths. You can paint each stick ½ red and ½ black.

Pattern in Brief
1. Single-pass 8, double-pass 6. Chorus: 1's sticks both inside.
2. In and out 6. Chorus: In and out 3.
3. Single-flip 12. Chorus: Double-flip R, L, single-flip center.
4. Double-flip 6. Chorus: Double-flip R, L, single-flip center.
5. Single-exchange 6, double-exchange 4. Chorus: Single-square 4 times.
6. Double-square. Chorus: Double-square. Flourish: 38.

Song

A   E papa wai rangi taku nei mahi
Taku nei mahi he taku ro-mata
E papa wai rangi taku nei mahi
Taku nei mahi he taku ro-mata.

B (Chorus) E aue ka mate au
E hine hoki i ho ra.

C   Maku E katue o hi-koi tanga
Maku E katue o hi-koi tanga.

D   Huri, huri, huri, huri, o mahara e
Ki te whai, ki te whai i te tau e
Kou rawa kou rawa o mahara e
Kia koe ra e hine, Kia koe ra e hine.

Pattern

Meas

1–4   Introduction, no movement.

          I (*music A*)

1   *Single pass:* Down (hit sticks on floor), together (hit sticks together), pass R stick to partner.

2   Down, together, pass L stick to partner.

3–8   Repeat single pass six more times (total of eight).

1–2   *Double pass:* Down, together, pass R stick to partner, pass R stick to partner. Down, together, pass L stick to partner, pass L stick to partner.

3–8   Repeat double pass (meas 1–2) four more times for total of six.

          First Chorus

1   *Sticks down* (ct 1), *hold* (ct 2–3).

2   *Sticks down* (ct 1), *hold* (ct 2), sticks down (ct 3).

3   (2/4 time for 1 meas.) Sticks together (ct 1), 1 pass both sticks on inside (ct 2) as 2 passes both sticks on outside (ct 2).

4–6   Repeat down (ct 1), together (ct 2), pass both (ct 3) (three times).

7—8   *Sticks down on ct 1, hold counts 2, 3, 4, 5, 6.*
(The italicized part of the chorus is the same in all
choruses. The center part can vary.)

II (*music C*)

1—8   *In and out*: Down (ct 1), together (ct 2), 1 pass both
sticks inside catching 2's sticks on outside (ct 3),
immediately return sticks on outside (ct 1) (or
where you caught them), and catch own sticks returning on inside. Remember to return sticks in
place you caught them. Total in and out is six.

Second Chorus

1—8   Down, 2, 3, down, 2, down (ct 3), together (ct 1), 1
throw in (2), and out (1), down (2), together (3), 1
throw in (1), and out (2), down (3), together (1),
throw in (2), and out (3), hold, 2, 3, 4, 5, 6.

III (*music A*)

1—2   *Single flip*: Hit tops of both sticks on floor on R
side; flip once, catching them in original position,
down in front, throw R. Repeat flip to L, down 2 in
front, and throw L.

3—16   Repeat for total of 12 times.

Third Chorus

1—8   Down, 2, 3, down, 2, hit tops of sticks down to R
(3), flip (1), flip (2), down center (1), pass R stick
(2), down to L (3), flip (1), flip (2), down center
(3), pass L stick (1), down center (2), single flip (3),
hold, 2, 3, 4, 5, 6.

IV (*music C*)

1   *Double flip*: Hit tops of both sticks to floor on R
side, flip twice, down in front, throw R.

2   Repeat to L side.

3—8   Repeat for total of six double flips.

Fourth Chorus

1—8   Repeat third chorus (double flip).

V (*music A*)

1   *Single exchange*: Hit sticks on floor, exchange sticks

between own hands, hit sticks on floor and pass R stick.

2   Repeat, passing L stick.

3—8   Repeat for total of 6 exchanges.

9—16   *Double exchange*: Repeat meas 1—8, exchanging sticks between hands twice for total of 4 exchanges and throws and 1 exchange without throw.

Fifth Chorus

1—8   Hold, 2, 3, hold, 2, hit sticks down (3), together (1), pass R straight across to partner (2), L to own R hand. This is done simultaneously. The path of sticks makes square pattern. Repeat square throw three times. Hold, 2, 3, 4, 5, 6. Count: Hold, 2, 3, hold, 2, down, together, square, down, together, square, down, together, square, down, together, square, hold, 2, 3, 4, 5, 6.

VI (*music C*)

1—8   *Double square*: Repeat square formation but throw R across and catch L in R hand, then reverse immediately: throw L across to partner, and catch R stick in L hand. Count: Down, together, square R, square L. Total of six double squares.

Sixth Chorus

1—8   Repeat chorus # 5 (square).

(*music D*)

1—16   *Flourish*: Listen for the spoken word, then hit sticks down, together; then continuously pass R, L, R, L for 38 times. If you drop sticks, start sequence with down, together, throw R.

Hints for Learning

First, practice the variations of stick passing. Someone count to keep the group together. First part: down, together, pass; second part: down, together, pass, pass. Demonstrate each pattern with the count. The call ahead for change of pattern can be done on the chorus holds. The rhythm of the chorus demands an unusual response. Hit sticks on floor on count one, hold 2, 3, hit the floor on count one, hold 2, hit on count one. Rhythm count: Down, 2, 3; down, 2; down, together, pass, etc.

Variation: Two couples in a small circle, partners facing diagonally. Couple 1 starts on ct 1 and couple 2 on ct 2. You can do single pass, single flip, single exchange, and single square.

7.
Learn
Costuming

Costumes add color and excitement to folk dances. Dance in a costume you have studied and designed yourself, and you will experience the thrill of creative achievement. A costume for folk dancing depicts authentically the outfit for a country, a class of people, or a period in history. This is one of the most challenging areas of research in the folk-dancing field. Seeing the actual costume is the greatest help you can get.

Authenticity in costuming is your goal as you research patterns, materials, and color combinations of materials. A native of a country is very proud of the costume or dress which represents his particular culture. Take time to do all these things correctly even though the expense may be a little more. Start with the costume of one country, a suite of dances, an enthusiastic group of dancers, and you will be on your way to experiencing new challenges in the folk dance.

The following costume plates were provided through the courtesy of the International Folk Dancers of Brigham Young University, Provo, Utah. Many of the costumes have been researched and designed by the students. The Hungarian, Philippine, and New Zealand costumes have come from those particular countries.

Vyts Beliajus, editor of *Viltis* magazine and fondly known as "Mr. Folk Dance of the United States," has contributed to the background material for each costume.

AMERICA

Research into our American history reveals many interesting outfits worn by men and women during different eras of our history. The costume used for the Western exhibition square dance is a modern dress. For the women, bright colors such as red and white in nylon organdy make colorful and durable dresses that hold up well for performance and travel. Cotton checks make an attractive outfit, with matching shirts for the men in the same pattern. A full petticoat and pantaloons complete the women's costume.

The men wear Western pants, a Western shirt with fringe, and cowboy boots. A trail tie is worn at the neck. The fringe can be purchased separately and sewed onto the men's shirt.

GERMANY

In Austria, Switzerland, and Bavaria you will see costumes similar to those in the costume plate. These three neighboring areas are located in the Alpine mountains. Bavaria, south of

Germany, was an independent kingdom until this century and has a distinct dialect. However, it is now a part of Germany, and the Alpine forms of the Schuhplattlers are the best-known dances to the general folk-dancing public.

The woman's outfit, known as the dirndl, has become so commonly worn that it may be either a housedress or a dressy outfit for folk dancing. The dresses shown were purchased in Germany.

The men's lederhosen come in colors of gray, green, or brown. The brown lederhosen are always plain, devoid of any embellishments. The green and gray, on the other hand, usually have embroidered floral designs and bone figures on the suspenders. The socks often worn with the lederhosen are very heavy-knit knee socks.

HUNGARY

The woman's costume shown here is from Kalocsa (Kah-loh-chah-ee) and is one of the most beautiful because of the elaborate hand embroidery on the apron, vest, and hat. The skirt is multipleated with either a solid color of red, pink, or blue, or a small floral design.

Kalocsa is on the left bank of the Danube River and south of Budapest. The Hungarian dances create an exciting movement of swirling skirts that show off the vivid embroidery of the dresses to good advantage.

The men wear the typical hussar (tightly fitting) trousers in white wool with designs of black braid on the front and across the back of the pants. The vest has buttons and is trimmed with braid.

The costume is elegant and dashing—the best known costume for folk dancers. The dresses in the costume plate are from Budapest. The women normally wear a loose-fitting slipper with no heel.

ISRAEL

The costume in the illustration was patterned after one worn by the Haifi dancers of Haifi, Israel. The costume is a red dress with sheafs of wheat appliqued of white material. The man wears white pants and a colored shirt to match the color of the woman's dress. The most typical colors worn by the Israeli performing groups are blue and white.

The Israeli costumes are still in the process of development. However, they are already beginning to take a recognizable form based somewhat on the Yemenite styles and what the Israelite dancers imagine were outfits worn in biblical days. These two sources are the main influences. However, the current styles for Israeli folk dancing should still be considered as "club costumes." Each demonstrational group or folk dance club selects a design and color scheme and adapts it to its needs and use.

LITHUANIA

Lithuanian costumes, no matter from which area, are easily recognizable. The aprons for the women may change drastically in design; the cut of the weskit may differ greatly; the patterns, in the woven designs or style of headgear, are distinct for regions. Some dresses may be of a plaid (languota) or of either horizontal or vertical stripes; yet, in spite of the differences they are similar and recognizable as Lithuanian.

The Lithuanian costumes are hand loomed. Each weaver expresses her artistry with her own interpretation of the acceptable designs of her area. Lithuanians rarely embroider,

and all floral or geometric designs are created during the weaving process. Therefore, making an imitation costume with materials obtainable in American fabric stores is next to impossible. The task is much easier for men's costumes where woven-in designs are at a minimum and solid colors can be used. The belt, or sash (juosta), is an essential part of the male gear. There are thousands of designs for these belts which are about 2½" wide and nearly three yards long with full "bearded" ends. The tie, also woven, is about 1—1½ inches wide and tied into a bowknot. The designs in the socks are usually knitted into the fabric, and the socks are fringed and worn over the trousers, which should blouse fully above the ankles.

117

MEXICO

Because of its great amount of folklore Mexico is a colorful country. Throughout Mexico a great variety of traditions, beliefs, music, dances, and costumes can be found. A reason for this variety is that different ethnic influences and geographical factors affect the personalities of the inhabitants. History, of course, is probably the main key to understanding Mexico.

Since the pre-Hispanic period we can observe a wide variety in the folklore of the country. There are many Indian groups, quite different from one another, although each one reflects certain influences from the Mayas or the Aztecs.

These two main groups reached a high level of civilization in different areas. They had high moral standards which they strongly emphasized in school. They had a considerable amount of knowledge in science as well as in the arts.

Before the Spaniards came, the Mayas and Aztecs not only had important drum beats but also flutes that added beauty to their original rhythms. During the 300 years of Spanish dominion, many changes took place. From the mixture of

118

Indian and Spanish cultures, an interesting variety of forms resulted. Racial, political, and ideological changes came to the actual Mexican folklore of today.

Every state in the republic has its own typical costume, music, steps, and choreography. Some states are rich in this manifestation of art, and it has been necessary to divide them into regions for a more profound study.

However, the country as a nation has a typical costume and a dance that are national and known worldwide.

The national dance is the Jarabe Tapatio known as the Mexican Hat Dance, pictured above.

The women must be in any bright color (pink, blue, orange, yellow, black, or white), with ribbons contrasting with the material. The fabric for the outfit can be cotton that is not too heavy, or taffeta that is not too sheer. The skirt should be knee length or a little longer. It should also be a circle and a half or preferably a double circle with a full slip of white cotton bordered around the bottom with points resembling scallops.

Under the slip white pantaloons are worn; they may be as plain or as fancy as desired. The slip should be almost the length of the skirt.

A shawl goes with the dress. Its color should contrast with the color of the dress or the ribbons. The common way to wear it is illustrated in the picture.

The hair style is usually two braids, with large bows where they begin and end, or a braided pony tail with bows.

Heavy jewelry is an important part of the costume: bracelets, earrings, and necklace. The earring is a circle of gold.

The men's national outfit is the charro, the typical costume of the state of Jalisco.

The picture shows sequins substituting for silver buttons. The jacket can have some ornament on the back, but it is also elegant if plain. The pants have either a double row of silver buttons along the outside or white braid. The sequins are for a theatrical appearance.

The national costume for the women is a long skirt with sequins covering most of the material. An eagle is the main figure. The dress is a manifestation of the skill and patience of the Mexican woman because it takes such a long time to make by hand. This costume should be worn only for the Jarabe Tapatio, but the dance can be performed in another costume like the one in the picture.

NEW ZEALAND

The original inhabitants of New Zealand are the Polynesians known as the Maoris (Mow-riz). With the coming of the white invaders their numbers were decimated. The *iwi* (tribes) that have survived still retain many customs. Their dance forms, for example, are very much alike.

Originally they wore a type of sarong woven from the New Zealand flax (*harakeke*). Now the popular dress for the Maori folk dancer is something akin to hula skirts made of hollow

reeds, usually of a natural color with black, red, and white designs reminiscent or their ancient tattoos or the designs around their meeting lodges.

PHILIPPINES

In a land composed of numerous islands and of a people consisting of diverse tribes and cultures, there are a great variety of costumes, from simple, primitive types to the elaborate, formal wear of Hispanic influence. However, the costume recognized by all folk dancers as Philippine is the dress with the butterfly shoulder sections for the women, the Maria Clara. For the men the airy see-through shirt of ecru and hand work of the same color down the front, the Barong Tagalog, is the most acceptable outfit for Tinikling.

POLAND

Since many of Poland's regions are dissimilar, the costumes are numerous and vary considerably from area to area—especially the costumes from extreme ends of the land. The best known Polish costume is the one from the Krakow region. The costume second in popularity is from Lowicz, pictured in the costume plate. It is of rainbow-striped woven material, short and full skirted. The material is easy to imitate and can be acquired in any dry goods store. The Lowicz costume is less lavish than the Krakowski and should not create problems in obtaining materials.

Normally, each regional dance requires the costume of that area. Obereks require the Lowicz costume, Mazurs and the Polonaise the more elegant costumes of the gentry; the Krakowiaks require Krakowski costumes, and the Mountaineers the Goral costume.

If you are to pick one costume to start your Polish wardrobe, the most feasible and least involved is the Lowicz costume, colorful and representative.

SCOTLAND

You need not look twice to know that kilts belong to Scotland. It is almost as national a symbol of the people as is the thistle. Because of nationalistic implications, the British at one time tried to prohibit the Scotsmen from wearing kilts. But the British did not succeed, and the lifting of the ban against kilts merited the creation of a dance to commemorate the event. The dance is called Sean Trubhais (Shawn Trews) which is popularly performed by all who do Scottish dancing.

The kilt, by right, is the costume for men. Traditional Scots frown upon women's wearing kilts except in Highland competition. The men also wear a velvet jacket. The dirk is a dagger worn in the sock legging, also an important part of the complete costume.

When women perform the strathspeys, they wear the country dress shown in the picture—a long white gown of formal attire.

UKRAINE

The Ukrainian homeland reaches from the Carpathian Mountains along the north shore of the Black Sea to the River Don and Kuban regions of the Caucasus. Basic apparel is similar throughout all regions, although each region has its own distinctive characteristics.

The Dneiper area costume is generally regarded as the most representative. In the women's costume, antiquity is preserved in the long blouse that becomes the dress. A beautiful Ukrainian motif is intricately embroidered on the wide sleeves, the neckline and bottom of the blouse in a cherry red and black. A heavy woven wool plaid skirt of cherry red and black with a wide opening at the front is tied around the waist and is known as the *plata*. A velvet apron decorated with richly embroidered ribbon is worn over the plaid skirt. The apron and coat are usually blue, wine, green, or black. A flared, sleeveless velvet jacket trimmed with rickrack is worn over the blouse. The head is adorned with a colorful floral wreath to which are attached ribbons that flow down the back. Several strands of red beads are always worn around the neck. The red leather boots make up an integral part of the costume.

The men's outfit consists of long wide-steppe trousers which blouse over the boots. The shirt is white with embroidery along the collar, down the front, and around the sleeve band. A wide sash is wound around the waist and tied so that the ends hang down at the left side. The popular colors of the Ukrainian costume are cherry red, blue, green, black, and orange.

Folk dancers should be extremely careful not to confuse the Ukrainian costumes with the Russian costumes.

BEGIN SIMPLY

Authenticity in costuming, as we have said, is the goal to strive for. And while you are building an adequate wardrobe, why not start with a few simple items?

To add color to an evening of folk dancing, the men can wear dark pants, white shirts, and a bright sash at the waist. The women can wear a bright colored skirt, a peasant blouse, and a black cummerbund at the waist. If the women are dressed alike, this costume presents a favorable picture for festival or club dancing.

There are many patterns for the woman's dirndl, representative of German and Austrian dances. For the men, a knicker pant or the lederhosen will compliment the women's costume. For a group just starting on costuming, the men may use bermuda shorts for the basic lederhosen. Then add straps to complete the costume.

Some clubs have had an initiation requirement for the women to make their own Ukrainian costume and cross-stitch their basic dress. With the addition of the plata, or backward apron (the basic apron), and a black coat you have started building your costume wardrobe. The men may start their costume with basic black pants and use them until they can obtain the baggy black pants typical of the Ukrainian and Russian costumes. For the shirts, a regular white shirt can be used. Sew it partway up the front; sew braid around the neck, down the front, and around the cuffs. For festival or exhibition dancing this costume will present a favorable picture.

Additional information on costuming can be obtained from the following sources:
1. The Folk Dance Federation of California publishes a calendar showing a different costume for each month. Address: Folk Dance Federation of California, 1095 Market Street, Room 213, San Francisco, California 94103.
2. *Viltis* and *Let's Dance* magazines have excellent illustrations of costuming. See "Folk Dance Magazines," following the bibliography, for addresses.
3. The *National Geographic* is one of the finest resource books on costuming. It includes color plates showing intricate detail.
4. Check to see if there are folk-dancing groups in your city or in cities nearby. Seeing an actual costume motivates you to get started.

Remember, begin with the costumes of one country and do a good job with those. Then move on to costumes of other countries.

8.
Take
Folk Dancing
out of the
Classroom

In what exciting ways can we enjoy folk dancing after we have learned the basic and beginning materials? This question presents numerous possibilities that will be discussed under the following headings: (1) Folk Dancing as a Performing Art, (2) Folk Dancing in European Festivals, and (3) Folk Dancing as a Lifetime Hobby.

FOLK DANCING AS A PERFORMING ART

When you enjoy the tremendous challenges of folk dancing, you naturally want to share this joy with other people. A folk dance performing ensemble is a means by which you may share the dancers' talents with audiences.

What must you consider before you are ready for performance work? Folk dancing is a living art, but it is also an art that has been handed down by the people of a country over the hundreds of years of the country's existence. Therefore, you must first be very sensitive to the authentic styling that is a part of the dances of a particular country. Furthermore, the costuming must be exact, and the dancers must represent in spirit and in movement the people's native culture. If you are performing a Ukrainian dance, for example, the styling is proud, exact, exciting, and demonstrative. The men must be vigorous and skillful, especially in their trick steps (prysiadkas), with the girls complementing the men at all times. The carriage of the body is tall with the toes and ankles extended in many of the steps. In contrast, as the same dancers do the Serbian silent kolo, the body settles down through the hips and the movements look heavier although the foot pattern is very light. The dance was traditionally performed in the fields or on dirt where the feet had to lift high enough not to stir up the dust. The silent kolo is called an "earthy dance" and is in direct contrast in many ways to the Ukrainian dances. The dancers' bodies must respond to yet another challenge of styling when they go up on "toe" for Scottish work. The erect body and formal movements of the feet and arms (very representative of balletic movement) give the dancers another definite change of styling that must be exact to make the dance representative of the area from which it originated. The styling for each dance does not stop with the body carriage and body movements, for such things as facial expressions help to transform the performers into Polish dancers, Hungarian dancers, or dancers from other countries.

When you perform your dances on stage, you are no longer dancing for your own pleasure alone. You are dancing to share that pleasure with your audience. Therefore, your choice of programming and your preparation are critical. If your program includes only three or four numbers as part of a larger program, then the "safety measure" is to present only exciting choreography that holds the interest of your audience. Conversely, when a full concert-length program of folk dance is presented, it can include some dances that are more unusual both rhythmically and technically. Some of these dances are typically more interesting to the dancers than to the audience.

Choice of musical accompaniment, recorded or live, is a major consideration and should not be treated lightly. In some cases you will find several musical arrangements for the same dance. Choose one that is pleasing to the ear and that carries the true spirit of the dance and of the people whom the dance represents. If the dance has fast, exciting movements, make sure your music supports this mood. The ability to select good musical accompaniment is one of the assets of a competent teacher or creative director.

Choreography is also a very important aspect of performance work. If you have had no experience with this phase of performance, it is advisable that you bring in a top specialist to teach performance material. Recognize, however, that controversy exists in the folk-dancing field over the subject of choreography. The controversy involves choreographic revisions of dances versus performance of dances in their original forms. The authors have found that in the international folk festivals of Europe, the majority of the outstanding performance groups use highly colorful choreography. You cannot change the basic step patterns in a folk dance and still retain authenticity. But you can use the basic step patterns in a

129

choreographical pattern that lends a beauty and an excitement otherwise lacking. For example, if a figure is repeated several times in a dance, it becomes boring to watch. To make more interesting choreography, combine three or four dances for one presentation with each dance figure repeated only a couple of times.

Often the question is asked: How do we learn exhibition dances? When you invite top specialists to teach your group, request a suite of dances representative of a region in the country of his specialty. Names of specialists are available from the magazines and record shops listed at the end of this book. Excellent choreography is worth the price if you plan to start a performing group. Start with the dances from one country. You will have the challenge of steps, styling, choreography, costuming, music, and the art of acquiring an ease in performance. Then add dances of a different country. When you are prepared to communicate a few dances to an audience, then try to gain experience in doing so. By this time you have developed competence as a performer of a core group of dances. Now the challenge is to expand, and there is no limit to how far your interests can carry you. An abundance of interesting dances exists worthy of presentation to audiences.

FOLK DANCING IN EUROPEAN FESTIVALS

"The world is our campus" is a statement that invites us to visit far-off places to learn more about the culture and customs of the people. The Orient, the Pacific Islands, Eastern Europe, and Western Europe each beckon us with promises of exciting experiences in the dance.

The old world is within the reach of many Americans. Scheduled tours and special charter flights beckon us to explore the old world—a world that holds fascinations of yesteryear and a touch-and-go acquaintance with the distant past. From the many exciting places to visit, let's choose Europe! Europe, where you can find either hundreds of local folk dance festivals featuring the natives of the country or the large international festivals that feature dancers from all over the world.

The practical question asked by the potential traveler is: "How do I know where to find information on when and where festivals are held in the different countries?" The first place to write is the tourist office of the largest city near the geographic area of your interest. For example, if you wish to attend festivals in Belgium, your first inquiry would be sent to Brussels, the capital city of the country. Also, *Viltis* magazine will furnish much information about European festivals. (See resource material at the end of this book.)

Let's mentally visit three of the large festivals in Europe to give you an idea of what you can expect. These festivals are representative of the hundreds that are held in Europe during the summer months of each year.

Schoten, located in a suburb of Antwerp, Belgium, is a very popular festival and is held during early July. The stage setting is beside a moat behind an ancient castle. The spectators enjoy the beauty of the natural setting as well as the highly professional performance by as many as thirty-five different dance groups. The flag-lined boulevard leading to the castle is the parade route that brings each of the performing groups before the public as they parade through the village. Each evening is highlighted by performances of top groups from around the world. The competition is keen, and the only rewards are acceptance and appreciation by the audience. An "after party" is held each evening where the participants become better acquainted and learn about each other's dances, music, costumes, and customs. True international understanding and friendship is the theme of the Schoten festival.

Dreams of attending a folk festival at the French Riviera on the shores of the Mediterranean can become a reality with the festival at Nice, France, held in the middle of July. Dance groups representative of countries around the world arrive for this exciting festival where the setting includes sightseeing along the Riviera and a trip along the sea to Monte Carlo for a look at the palace of Prince Rainier and Princess Grace of Monaco.

The performing area is in an open amphitheater along the Promenade des Anglais, located just across the boulevard from a beach on the Mediterranean. Typical of the performing groups are representatives from Sweden, Spain, Italy, Congo, Belgium, England, Ireland, Bulgaria, Romania, Yugoslavia, Turkey, Hungary, France, Switzerland, USA, and Czechoslovakia. Each group is given approximately nine minutes per performance. Truly a kaleidoscope of color and movement greets the eyes of the spectators. Parades are always part of the festival. The parades in Nice end at the Grand Square where each group does a brief performance before the dignitaries of the city and the hundreds of spectators that gather in the square.

If your taste for European beauty centers around an Alpine setting, the festival at Tarcento, Italy, shares with you the beauties of a charming village nestled at the foot of the Italian Alps only a few miles from the Yugoslavian Alps. The most unique part of this festival is a fantastically beautiful stage setting. The beautiful chateaus, nestled among the trees and blended into the hillside, form a backdrop that reaches toward the sky. The program starts in darkness; then each country is presented on stage. The lighting becomes more dramatic with the introduction of each additional group. At the completion of the introduction and with all of the performers on stage, all of the chateaus on the hill behind the stage become brilliantly lighted, and this marks the opening of the festival.

Each country presents dances representative of its culture, and each group is requested to do only the dances of its own country. The live music fills the night air with sounds ranging from Western hoedown music from the USA to a formal orchestral presentation by the Hungarian ensemble featuring ten violinists in a company of fourteen.

International folk dance festivals are held in every country in

Europe. To make folk-dancing experiences as meaningful, creative, and exciting as possible you should become a participant of or at least a visitor to some of these folk festivals.

FOLK DANCING AS A LIFETIME HOBBY

A hobby is a pursuit outside one's regular occupation engaged in for relaxation and enjoyment. Folk dancing could develop into a life long hobby for you either as a performer or as one interested in studying the dances and the cultures from which they developed.

As you learn the Hopak, the national dance of the Ukraine, the intense vitality and joy of the dance stimulates within you an interest to know more about the culture from which it came. This dance features the men with such vigorous and challenging skills as the prysiadkas, and the women compliment the men with fast, light, and exact movements. The balalaika, a musical instrument associated with Russia, is the main accompaniment for Ukrainian songs and dances. The modern instrument has three strings running down a long neck. Only the first and third strings are used, since the middle string is left to echo the vibrations.

Since 1971 the Russians have offered a tremendous opportunity to find out what life is really like in the Soviet Union. With these new opportunities, many people will be able to visit Russia. But if you cannot actually go there, with the help of resource materials you can sit in an armchair and mentally visit Moscow with the golden-domed cathedrals where Russian czars were crowned. You can visit the Palace of Congress, Ivan the Great's Bell Tower, and the Armoury Museum where the jeweled treasures of Czarist Russia—from thrones to carriages—are on display. A visit to Kiev directs you toward the Vladimir Hills overlooking the Dnieper River. The group of Kiev Pechera monasteries rising on the hills along the river is another fascinating stop. This vast complex of buildings, once a shrine, is now a museum with a spectacular collection of Ukrainian folk art, carvings, ceramics, and embroidery. The Kiev ballet is a must for the evening entertainment—to see their magnificent presentation of the "Hopak." Your hobby has just started, leading you to a lifetime of reading and research that will bring the world to your doorstep through the media of folk dancing and its underlying cultures.

G. Stanley Hall stated that whenever members of alien primitive tribes sought closer acquaintance with each other they asked a single question in sign language: "What do you dance?" And as these respective members performed their dances, answering the question, each became acquainted with the other. (*Encyclopaedia Britannica*.) In the process of time, primitive tribes evolved into the separate nations which comprise the modern world. Each nation then developed its particular folk dances stemming from this common heritage of primitive man.

Folk dancing gives us much insight into the history and national character of the people of a country. Let folk dancing add to your understanding of people from other countries; let it add to your personality and your enjoyment.

9.
Test and
Evaluate Your
Knowledge

In any field of endeavor, a feeling of accomplishment is very important. The following tests will guide you in judging your personal achievement in the field of folk dance.

A. Identify the nationality of each by choosing the proper number from the column below.

1. ___ Alunelul		1. African
2. ___ Corrido		2. American
3. ___ Cotton-eyed Joe		3. Czechoslovakian
4. ___ Czardas Vengerka		4. Danish
5. ___ D'Hammerschmiedsg'selln		5. English
6. ___ Doudlebska Polka		6. Estonian
7. ___ Ersko Kolo		7. German
8. ___ Galopede		8. Greek
9. ___ Hambo		9. Hungarian
10. ___ Hier Ek Weer		10. Irish
11. ___ Hopak		11. Israeli
12. ___ Jessie Polka		12. Lithuanian
13. ___ Kalvelis		13. Mexican
14. ___ Korobushka		14. New Zealand
15. ___ Kreuz Koenig		15. Philippine
16. ___ Lech Lamidbar		16. Polish
17. ___ Lowland Schottische		17. Romanian
18. ___ Maori Stick Game		18. Russian
19. ___ Mayim, Mayim		19. Scandinavian
20. ___ Misirlou		20. Scottish
21. ___ Oslo Waltz		21. Scotch-English
22. ___ Pod Borem		22. Swedish
23. ___ Raksi Jaak		23. Ukrainian
24. ___ Road to the Isles		24. Yugoslavian (Serbian)
25. ___ Salty Dog Rag		
26. ___ Sauerlander Quadrille		
27. ___ Shepherd's Crook		
28. ___ Sweets of May		
29. ___ Tant' Hessie		
30. ___ Tinikling		
31. ___ To Tur		
32. ___ Uzicka Carlama		
33. ___ Vayiven Uziyahu		
34. ___ Ve' David		
35. ___ Ziogelis		

B. Name the basic step for the following dances. (Example: *Polka*: Doudlebska Polka)

 1. ___ Hier Ek Weer
 2. ___ Tant' Hessie
 3. ___ Cotton-Eyed Joe
 4. ___ To Tur
 5. ___ Sauerlander Quadrille
 6. ___ Kalvelis
 7. ___ Ziogelis
 8. ___ Corrido
 9. ___ Korobushka
10. ___ Shepherd's Crook

C. Match the formations described above with the basic dance positions listed below.

1. ___ Single circle, dancers moving L
2. ___ Single circle, dancers moving R
3. ___ Partners facing same direction, cross hand hold
4. ___ W's hands on M's shoulders M's hands on W's waist
5. ___ Partners standing R hips together
6. ___ Partners, M on inside of circle W on outside, both facing CCW
7. ___ Partners, M holding W's hands R in R, L on L shoulder high
8. ___ Face partner, M's R hand on W's waist, W's R hand in M's L hand

1. Closed ballroom position
2. Counterclockwise direction
3. Varsouvienne position
4. Promenade position
5. Clockwise direction
6. Square dance swing position
7. Double circle
8. Shoulder-waist position

Test and Evaluate Your Knowledge

D. Match the basic step patterns with their names.

1. ___ Polka	1.	Toe, toe, heel, toe, side, behind, bounce
2. ___ Schottische	2.	Hop, step, close, step
3. ___ Waltz	3.	Step, step, step, hop
4. ___ Two-Step	4.	Side, behind, side, in front
5. ___ Grapevine	5.	Step, step, close
6. ___ Neheimer Step	6.	Step, close, step

E. Name eight leaders in the folk dance field and the nationality of the dances that have made them prominent (check dance descriptions and bibliography). Example: Vyts Beliajus, Lithuanian Dances

Answers

Section A

1. *17*, 2. *13*, 3. *2*, 4. *9*, 5. 7, 6. *3*, 7. *23*, 8. *5*, 9. *22*, 10. *1*, 11. *23*, 12. 2, 13. *12*, 14. *18*, 15. 7, 16. *11*, 17. *19*, 18. *14*, 19. *11*, 20. 8, 21. *21*, 22. *16*, 23. *6*, 24. *20*, 25. 2, 26. 7, 27. *20*, 28. *10*, 29. *1*, 30. *15*, 31. *4*, 32. *24*, 33. *11*, 34. *11*, 35. *12*.

Section B
1. Walk, 2. Walk, 3. Polka, 4. Two-step, 5. Neheimer step, 6. Polka, 7. Two-step, 8. Grapevine, 9. Schottische, 10. Waltz.

Section C
1. *5*, 2. 2, 3. *4*, 4. *8*, 5. *6*, 6. 7, 7. *3*, 8. *1*.

Section D
1. *2*, 2. *3*, 3. *5*, 4. *6*, 5. *4*, 6. *1*.

138

Glossary

Arch:
> *Couple Arch:* One couple holds hands high as second couple goes under arch.
>
> *R arch high, L go under:* In sets of 3s, person in center holds R hand high, forming an arch with W on his R. The L W goes under arch as two W change places.

Back-Skaters' Position: Hands are held behind backs with partners facing same direction. M holds W's L hand in his L, W's R hand in his R. L arms are on top.

Balance:
> *Waltz Balance:* Step L fwd (ct 1), close R to L and hold (ct 2-3).
>
> *Two-Step Balance:* Step L fwd (ct 1), step R beside L (ct 2), step L in place (ct 3).

Ball Change: See *Change Weight.*

Bokazo: Hop on L ft and point R toe fwd, heel slightly turned in (ct 1), hop on L ft and place R ft beside L, heels of both feet slightly turned out (ct 2), with sharp clicking movement close R heel to L heel (ct 3), and hold (ct 4).

Change Weight (Ball Change): Step R, step on ball of L ft, and immediately step back to R ft.

Chase: One dancer follows same course as another dancer.

Cherkassiya: Used in Israeli dancing to mean same as grapevine. Cross R over L, step L to L side, cross R behind L, step L to L side.

Chug: See *Push Step.*

Clicks: Raise R ft about 8 inches to side while hopping and lifting L ft up to touch R ft.

Cuddle: As partners hold inside hands, W on R, W makes L turn into M's arm. Her L arm is across her waist holding M's R hand.

Cut Step: Change weight to L ft and extend R ft fwd.

Do-Sa-Do: Facing partner, walk fwd passing R shoulder, and return to place, walking bwd and passing L shoulder.

Elbow Swing: Partners hook R elbows and turn cw.

Glossary

Figure Eight: Couples facing, M touch L hands, cross over and turn opposite W with R hand, M touch L hands and cross back to place and turn partner with R hand.

Grand Right and Left: Facing partner, clasp R hands and pull her by; take next girl with L hand, pull her by; continue, R hand then L hand, around circle.

Grapevine: L ft back of R, R ft to R, L ft in front of R, R ft to R.

Grasshopper Step: Start with R ft; dance fwd with 2 two-steps. Finish second by bending L knee in fwd dip. Starting with R ft, do 2 two-steps bwd, ending with bwd dip. As you dip fwd, body leans fwd. As you dip bwd, body leans bwd.

Hambo Turn: M stamps R, turning inward toward partner, taking closed dance position. W steps L, moving into closed position. M steps L in sideward movement as W touches R toe behind L foot. M touches R toe beside L foot, W steps R.

Highland Fling and Rock Step: In line of 3 facing forward, hop L, pt R to side, hop L, pt R behind calf, hop L, pt R to side, hop L, pt R in front of calf. Put weight on ball of R ft directly in front of L ft as you touch L toe directly behind R ft. Rock back on ball of L ft, pt R toe directly in front of L. Repeat rock fwd on R, back on L.

Highland Fling Step: 3 Highland fling steps beginning with hop on L and pointing R: Hop L, pt R to side, hop L, pt R ft behind calf, hop L, pt R ft in front of calf, hop L, pt R ft behind calf. Repeat twice. M continue into fourth highland fling, pt L to side, make a complete R turn as pt behind, in front, behind calf. W take 4 walking steps making a R turn (cw) in individual circles.

King's Cross: M, facing slightly to L, take 8 running steps fwd moving cw. W, acting as pivot point, run in place with slight kick fwd. During next 4 running steps, M release W's L hands and pull with their R, exchanging places with W. Repeat with M back to back in center. Repeat entire dance.

Landler Step: Step L with slightly bent knee, step R, then L, on toes. Pattern follows: Down, up, up (¾ time).

Lunge Step: Step diagonally fwd on R ft, bending knee; cut-step fwd with L ft displacing R ft, run fwd R, L, R.

Mazurka: Step L ft diagonally L fwd, bring R ft to L with cut step, hop on R ft and bring L ft across R leg in quick out-in movement. The count is step, close, hop.

Neheimer: See *Sauerlander Quadrille.*

Pas de Basque: Leap diagonally R with R ft (ct 1), step on L toe in front of R ft (ct &), shift weight to R ft (cts 2, &).

Pivot turn: Complete turn on R ft, step fwd on L for R pivot turn.

Prysiadka: Typical Russian men's squat steps used to show strength of male dancer (never performed by women).
1. With bent knees, squat to floor settling just above heels. Alternately kick R ft fwd, then L ft fwd.
2. Jump into air spreading legs to split position, touching toes with fingertips.
3. In deep-knee squat position, jump on both feet; then jump onto L ft and extend R leg straight to side; repeat, alternating 4 steps L, then 4 steps R.

Push Step: With weight on R ft, bring L toe to instep of R ft and push R ft to R side.

Scottish Reel of Three: In line of 3, M and W 1 face; W 2 faces toward M. Starting with R ft, all travel 8 strathspey steps, making figure 8. W 2 dances one step in place before becoming part of figure 8. Pass R shoulder first. (In Figure 8 always pass R shoulder on R side of set and L on L side of set.)

Seesaw: Facing partner, walk fwd passing L shoulder, and return to place, walking bwd and passing R shoulder.

Sevens and Threes: See *Sweets of May*.

Shepherd's Crook: M and W on L form arch for W 1 to go under and return to place, using 4 strathspey steps. M & W 2 dance in place and on third step the man follows W 1 under arch. On fourth step W 2 turns R under her R arm. This entire movement is large.

Russian Polka: Leap fwd on R, run fwd L, R, leap fwd on L, run fwd R, L. Keep feet lifts very close to floor. Make movement smooth.

Soldado: This figure represents cutting of a piece of pie. M start with R ft, back into center with 4 walking steps. M leads diagonally L out of center with 4 walking steps. Repeat this figure three times. On the third time coming out of center, M steps L, stamps R, L.

Star: Join R or L hand (as designated) in center of couple or couples.

Step-Draw: Step L to L side, draw R ft along floor to L ft.

Strathspey Rocking Step: Beginning R, step fwd R, hop R, step back L, hop L, grapevine to the L, stepping R ft behind, L ft to side, R ft diagonally L in front and hop R.

Strathspey Step: Step fwd R, close L to R, step fwd R, lift R heel slightly as L ft swings through and reaches fwd for next step. Knees are turned out at all times.

Three-Step Turn: From position facing center, step R to R

turning body to face ccw (ct 1), step to L completing R turn (ct 2), step R to R (ct 3), hold (ct 4).

Tinikling Step: Standing on L side of poles, R shoulder to poles, hop on L ft outside poles, leap between poles R, L, leap to R side of poles on R ft, leap between poles L, R.

Toe-Heel, Cross-Kick: Hop on L ft, touch R toe to side (knee turned in); hop on L ft, touch R heel in same place R toe was touched; hop on L ft and touch R toe in front of L ft; hop on L ft and kick R ft diagonally fwd.

Touch, Kick, Run-2-3: Hop on L ft and touch R ft at side of L ankle, hop on L ft and extend R ft fwd about 8 inches from floor, then run fwd, R, L, R.

Weathervane: Two couples facing, W on M's R. M move fwd to hook L elbows, reaching behind M to take opposite W's L hand. M's R arm is around partner's waist.

Bibliography

Beliajus, V. F. *Dance and Be Merry*. Vols. 1-2. Chicago: Clayton F. Summy Co., 1940.

_____ *The Dance of Lietuva.* Chicago: Clayton F. Summy Co.

Burchenal, Elizabeth. *Folk Dances and Singing Games*. New York: G. Schirmer, 1922.

_____. *Folk Dances of Germany*. New York: G. Schirmer, 1938.

Czarnowski, Lucille. *Folk Dance Teaching Cues*. Stockton, California: University of Pacific Folk Dance Camp, 1961.

Duggin, Anne, Jeanette Schlottman, and Abbie Rutledge. *Folk Dance of European Countries* and *The Teaching of Folk Dance*. New York: A. S. Barnes and Co., 1948.

Dunsing, Gretel and Paul. *Dance Lightly*. Delaware, Ohio: Co-operative Recreation Service, 1946.

Folk Dance Federation of California, Inc. *Folk Dances From Near and Far, International Series*. Vols. 1-8, Vols. A, B, C, A_2, B_2. San Francisco: Folk Dance Federation of California, 1095 Market Street, Room 213.

Fox, Grace I. and Kathleen G. Merrill. *Folk Dancing in High School and College*. New York: A. S. Barnes and Co., 1944.

Hall, J. Tillman. *Dance! A Complete Guide to Social, Folk, and Square Dancing*. Belmont, California: Wadsworth Publishing Company, 1963.

Herman, Michael. *Folk Dances For All*. New York: Barnes and Noble, 1947.

Jensen, Clayne R. and Mary Bee. *Square Dancing*. Provo, Utah, Brigham Young University: Young House, 1973.

Joukowsky, Anatol M. *The Teaching of Ethnic Dance*. New York: J. Lowell Pratt & Co.

Kraus, Richard. *Folk Dancing*. New York: The Macmillan Co., 1962.

Lapson, Dvora. *Dances of the Jewish People*. New York: The Jewish Education Committee, 1954.

LaSalle, Dorothy. *Rhythms and Dances for Elementary Schools*. New York: A. S. Barnes and Co., 1926.

Lawson, Joan. *European Folk Dances—Its National and Musical Characteristics*. New York: Pitman Publishing Co.

Lidster, Miriam D. and Dorothy H. Tamburini. *Folk Dance Progressions*. Belmont, California: Wadsworth Publishing Co., 1965.

Tolentino, Francisco Reyes. *Philippine National Dances*. New York: Silver Burdett Co., 1946.

Folk Dance Shops and Camps

FOLK DANCE RECORDS AND BOOK SHOPS

V. F. Beliajus: P.O. Box 1226, Denver, Colo. 80201

Festival Records: 161 Turk Street, San Francisco, Calif. 94102

Festival Records: 2769 West Pico, Los Angeles, Calif. 90006

Folklore Center: 4100 University Way, Seattle, Wash. 98109

Folk Music International: 56-40 187 Street, Flushing, N.Y. 11365

Folkraft: 1159 Broad Street, Newark, N.J. 07114

Michael Herman's Folk Dance House: P.O. Box 201, Flushing, N.Y. 11352

International Record Industries, Inc.: 135 W. 41st Street, New York, N.Y. 10036

Monitor Recordings, Inc.: 156 Fifth Avenue, New York, N.Y. 10010

FOLK DANCE MAGAZINES

Let's Dance: c/o Folk Dance Federation of California, Inc. 1095 Market Street, Rm. 213, San Francisco, Calif. 94103

Viltis: P.O. Box 1226, Denver, Colo. 80201

FOLK DANCE CAMPS AND SUMMER SCHOOLS

Folk dance camps are generally found on the West and East coasts. If you can attend one of these camps, you will have the opportunity to work with top leaders in the folk dance field. Most of the instructors are from the country of the dances they are teaching, or they have recently studied in Europe. For any folk dance teacher it is a must to attend one of the following camps for an unforgettable experience of folk dancing at its finest.

Western Folk Dance Camps

FOLK DANCE CAMP, UNIVERSITY OF THE PACIFIC, STOCKTON, CALIF. Jack B. McKay, Director.

IDYLLWILD FOLK DANCE WORKSHOP, Information from Elma McFarland, 144 S. Allan Ave., Pasadena, Calif. 91106

INTERNATIONAL FOLK DANCE CAMP, The Lighted Lantern Foundation, Route 5, Box 825, Golden, Colo. 80401

MENDOCINO FOLKLORE CAMP, Information from Nancy Linscott, 40 Glen Drive, Mill Valley, Calif. 94941

SAN DIEGO STATE COLLEGE FOLK DANCE CONFERENCE, San Diego State College, San Diego, Calif. 92115

Eastern Folk Dance Camps

FOLKDANCE INSTITUTE OF NEW YORK, Mosche Eskayo Folk Dance Institute, 99 Hillside Avenue, New York, N.Y. 10023

ISRAELI FOLK DANCE WORKSHOP, Blue Star Folk Dance Workshop, 1104 Crescent Ave., N.E., Atlanta, Ga. 30309

KENTUCKY DANCE INSTITUTE, Morehead State University. Shirley Durham, 4540 Southern Parkway, Louisville, Ky. 40214

Index